Crowning Conversations

Deidra Ewing M.A.

Yvette *"Genesis Blu"* Cornish, MA, LPC

Patrina *"Mz. Ann"* Randolph, CLC, BFA

Felishia Brown, CLC, BA

ARCHWAY PUBLISHING

This book is a work of non-fiction. Unless otherwise noted, the author
and the publisher make no explicit guarantees as to the accuracy of
the information contained in this book and in some cases, names of
people and places have been altered to protect their privacy.

Archway Publishing books may be ordered through booksellers or by contacting:

Archway Publishing
1663 Liberty Drive
Bloomington, IN 47403
www.archwaypublishing.com
844-669-3957

Because of the dynamic nature of the Internet, any web addresses or
links contained in this book may have changed since publication and
may no longer be valid. The views expressed in this work are solely those
of the author and do not necessarily reflect the views of the publisher,
and the publisher hereby disclaims any responsibility for them.

Any people depicted in stock imagery provided by Getty Images are models, and
such images are being used for illustrative purposes only.
Certain stock imagery © Getty Images.

Unless otherwise noted, scripture taken from the King James Version of the Bible.

Scripture quotations marked MSG are taken from THE MESSAGE,
copyright © 1993, 2002, 2018 by Eugene H. Peterson. Used by permission
of NavPress, represented by Tyndale House Publishers. All rights reserved.

Scripture quotations marked (AMP) taken from the
Amplified® Bible (AMP), Copyright © 2015 by The Lockman
Foundation. Used by permission. www.lockman.org

All Scripture marked with the designation "GW" is taken from GOD'S WORD®.
© 1995, 2003, 2013, 2014, 2019, 2020 by God's Word to
the Nations Mission Society. Used by permission.

Scripture quotations marked (NLT) are taken from the Holy
Bible, New Living Translation, copyright ©1996, 2004, 2015 by
Tyndale House Foundation. Used by permission of Tyndale House
Publishers, Carol Stream, Illinois 60188. All rights reserved.

ISBN: 978-1-6657-0918-7 (sc)
ISBN: 978-1-6657-0920-0 (hc)
ISBN: 978-1-6657-0919-4 (e)

Library of Congress Control Number: 2021913343

Print information available on the last page.

Archway Publishing rev. date: 11/03/2021

CONTENTS

FOREWORD

I've never been a person who was given shit. I've always had to work extra hard for anything I wanted. As such, I have had so many crowning moments that I've lost count. Yes, I'm a mother, daughter, instructor, entrepreneur, and the wife of celebrity rapper Paul Wall, but I'm really so much more. So what happens to a dream deferred?

I decided to drop out of college my junior year due to stress and extreme pressure from my parents. I was working three jobs while trying to be a successful student. I had accumulated so much debt in student loans even though I really had no idea what I wanted to be. I knew that I loved to sing and even beat out the future Beyonce in a talent show as a kid. I was quickly thrusted into the entertainment industry, which I found out was mostly bullshit. I was in a musical group for about four years that was extremely demanding. At one point, I was even tasked with choosing between living with my parents and staying with the group. My parents wanted me to stay in school and live a normal life, but I had bigger plans. So I left the home of my sheltering parents because I wanted to be a team player and moved in with my other two group members and their parents. They worked us to the bone so we could compete with groups like Destiny's Child. We weren't allowed to have jobs or associate with the outside world if it didn't involve the group. I had tunnel vision, so I couldn't see it until it was too late. At one point, I genuinely felt trapped; that's when Paul came along. There I was faced with another crowning moment. I decided to leave the home and eventually the group. Even though I moved in with Paul and things were going well, I fell into a deep depression. I felt that I had let the other group members down and had given up on my dream. Things eventually turned around as I stayed involved with music by singing background for celebrities such as Scarface.

I now realize that it was imperative to remove myself from that toxic environment if I ever wanted to move forward and have peace. Although it hurt like hell and felt like the wrong choice at the time, it wasn't. Happiness found me with Paul and our family, but another crowning moment was waiting right around the corner.

After having a child, I gained about one hundred pounds, which was a shock for me; I had never been that size. This turned about to be a greater issue, as my family helped me cultivate body image issues since they focused on weight and made comments all the time. For example, my aunt, who is small, would constantly express her concern about getting fat. I began to focus on this as well, which led to a complex. In addition, my now husband, Paul, also gained about one hundred pounds with each pregnancy. We were essentially living a very unhealthy rapper lifestyle, which included eating fast foods, drinking alcohol, and even popping pills. We were in our twenties and were millionaires, so you can imagine the things we did. To add stress, we had several family members leaning on us for assistance. Paul had gotten up to about 330 pounds and lost no weight even after running three miles a day. He was eventually diagnosed with high blood pressure, which terrified me. After our last child, we decided to have weight-loss surgery. I opted for liposuction. I immediately felt back to the self I knew. I was back to being snatched, which gave me a self-esteem boost. This was temporary, however, as I realized that I had been conditioned to equate a hot body with self-worth and self-love.

Years later, I was back to being overweight because … I'm an "eataholic." We hadn't changed our eating habits, so it was easy to fall back into the same routine. Unfortunately, each time I lost weight, it would come back twice as hard, leaving me experiencing bouts of depression periodically. I was stuck in a vicious cycle, as food was often the way to comfort and console myself through those depressive episodes. I recently, through reflection, learned that this is directly related to the interactions with women in my family. We don't show affection in the traditional way; instead, I was shown love and concern through cooked meals. It was not "let me hug you" but "let me feed you."

Things started to change for the better when we moved to California, which allowed me to really focus on my fitness journey with little to no distractions. After three years, my husband decided it was time to go home. I dreaded this, as I knew we would have to go back to taking care of other people and being exposed to unhealthy environments. I gained weight almost immediately and was back to two hundred pounds. I was uncomfortable in my skin. It was clear that my ability to thrive was directly connected to my environment. I've learned that it is difficult to heal in the place you were hurt.

An opportunity presented itself, in which I participated—a documentary where celebrity rappers and their families discussed the importance of healthy eating and living. At this time, I loved my husband but was starting to get over being "Paul Wall's wife." I had other goals besides just being somebody's wife. I was very independent and always wanted my own. If I'm being honest, I did get comfortable with having somebody take care of me and not having to work myself to the bone as I had done previously. I had attempted reality TV, but it was obvious that I wasn't cut out for that life and would not pretend to be someone I am not.

After the documentary interview, I was hired to be a blogger for a health and fitness blog. I had gained expertise in portion control, meal prep, and more while living in California. At the same time, I began taking Zumba classes and fell in love with it. I was able to lose forty pounds doing Zumba regularly. I decided to start a fitness group with some of my friends, and we really inspired and motivated one another. I learned from them that you can lead with compassion, have fun, and make people feel comfortable even about weight loss and fitness. It didn't have to be a negative experience. We encouraged others no matter what size they were and where they were in their fitness journey. I feel that women need that; we don't need to go somewhere and be shamed for our bodies or appearance. We really have enough of that in the world.

I started teaching Zumba and hosting free classes. It became such a hit that we would pack the room. I realized it was something women really wanted and needed. My mission at this time was to break the cycle, which became my hashtag. At one point, I had more teaching jobs than I could count on my hand. Back to working to the bone. This changed when I settled at one studio and was able to create a big enough clientele to leave my other gigs.

This gave birth to my brand and company, so around 2013, I was able to open my own studio, MixFitz, where I was able to help myself and many other women break the cycle.

I learned the importance of the holistic approach to success and happiness. I try to address my spirituality by tapping into the God in me and trusting it. If God is an infinite source, then it exists in abundance and lives within you. We all have infinite abundance in us; we just have to tap in. So I choose to get away from the distractions and tap.

After my sister passed away in 2014, my family experienced a huge transition. This was at the same time of having another baby. I was at the top of my game, and my business was thriving. Funny how life can come along and knock you off of your high horse. The death of my sister was very traumatic, but as taught in my family, with didn't show it. So I ate, and my emotions showed through my weight gain again. This time around though, I decided to take care of my mental health. It was always my MO to push through the pain, but an unexpected death is something you can't just push through. You are forced to heal or stay broken. You cannot rush the healing but instead must work to find peace. This was a defining moment, and I learned how to find peace and comfort in a way that was good for my mental and physical health. It took about two years, but I succeeded.

Now, my family of four and I have moved to a secluded area where no one can just roll up on us. This is actually the first time we have not had any other family members or friends living with us. I have gone through grief, pain, struggles, and even relationship turmoil, and one of the most helpful things was to check myself. This is something that I continue to do, admitting that sometimes I'm a part of the problem and am not above reproach. Finally, I realized that my happiness depends on me.

I am so excited to provide the foreword for this book, as I greatly identified with the core concepts the women discuss. I want to stress the importance for every woman to take the time to read this book and understand that you are not alone, you deserve to heal, and you deserve to have your dreams come true. You will also be able to recognize that the struggles and pain are a part of the game, and learning how to pick yourself back up is the key. This book provides real-life examples of how women like myself have done this, and it explains exactly how they did it! This is a book that you will want to get together and discuss with friends. Remember to do your shadow work so you can get back to the light.

—Crystal Wall

INTRODUCTION

The Perfect Woman to Crowning Conversations

We want to emphasize the title of this book. What you are about to read is a full-blown crowning conversation. It's a humble moment from our crown to yours to remind you that you are not alone in this journey. This book was almost named *A Conversation for the Culture*, which still stands true, but there's something about the image of you holding your head up and wearing your crown that is piercing to our souls. After reading this, we envision you with your back straight, confidence lifted, strong in the face of adversity, and beautifully embracing the scars life has given you. We picture you perfect. We picture you the *perfect woman*.

Throughout life, whether it be conversations with our friends and family or different posts and happy images that flood our time lines, a crowning conversation is an outpouring of the things most people don't talk about. It's unapologetic, bold, and powerful talk about life events that could have broken you, yet you're still pushing—pushing through trauma, pushing through stress, pushing through having a skin color some people may hate, and pushing through to become the best version of yourself. The crowned queens who wrote this book understand what it means to go above and beyond excuses and hate. We understand that what could have been a setback was a setup for success. We understand that the person reading this is either broken or has been broken before, so we invite you into the circle with gratitude, caution, and care. You can sit with us. We want you to know that despite anything that has ever happened to you, we get it, and you're not alone.

Crowning conversations are the unfiltered truths you deserve to hear—from the hardcore, arm-locked, sis-get-back-up, judgment-free, unapologetic sisterhood you've been waiting for. It's something like the Greek life. It's a day to be celebrated. Our colors are black and blue, and our battle stance is a face lifted to the heavens with eyes closed and arms uplifted as a representation of freedom. CC—established in 2021. Our oath is a commitment to reflect on the pieces of life that require physical, mental, and spiritual authenticity, which is often lacking within our community. This is the book you want to read and the book you deserve to read.

As you read through what each author decided to share, we want you to think about how you identify with each of us. We want you to write down how the perfect imperfections shared help make you perfect too. We want to hear from you. As this book provides you with what you need to move forward, we also pray that this message stirs you up enough to take action on what's been holding you back from moving forward. We invite you to a fallout with a modesty cloth as you decide to pursue the gifts and talents embedded in you after reading this. Your life will be explosive if you apply these lessons. Grab your girlfriends for happy hour, a pajama night in, or a virtual meeting to talk through your hard spots. You don't have to get through this season alone. You don't have to carry the weights of life by yourself. It's going to be hard hitting the reset button on yourself, but this is your time. This is the sign you've been looking for.

PART 1

It Levels to This

EMPTY

So far, I've survived growing up in a dysfunctional home, learning what it means to be an addict, being a firsthand witness to a mental health disorder, watching my mom raise a family of four on a teacher's salary, turning my back on God, and being addicted to anything that made me feel better—whether it was drugs, money, sex, or alcohol. I've survived divorced parents, abusive relationships, postpartum depression, a perfectly planned suicide, the weight of homelessness, embarrassment, the deaths of loved ones, self-diagnosed anxiety, a borderline overdose, COVID-19, and too many nights of "What the heck happened last night?" You know, a little bit of nothing.

I could write a whole other book about my past. I've seen and done so much that I live a judgment-free life. It took me a while to get to this point, but I now understand that everything that someone does on the outside has everything to do with what is going on on the inside. Sometimes I have conversations with people, and they share their darkest secrets with me, and I'm just sitting there like

"Girl, I get it." And I mean it. Sincerely. I'm the furthest thing from perfect, although I look like nothing of what I've been through. I've lost the woman in the mirror more times than I can count, but I've never stopped at least attempting to become the best version of myself. I want to help you with that too. I used to have this horrible habit of focusing on everything that was wrong with me. Physically speaking, it was always my weight or my crooked teeth. Mentally, it was beating myself up for past mistakes. Spiritually, it was knowing that I should be doing more with my life but not being able to fully trust in the Lord like church folk tried to tell me to. I had to stop focusing on what was wrong with me and begin focusing on what was right with me.

Despite my own choices and uncontrolled upbringing, I want my kids and you to know that I get whatever it is life throws your way. What I want to help with are the excuses we use to justify our actions. In most cases, we know better. We just choose not to do better for whatever reason.

Let's think about it.

How healthy is it to think anything less than greatness about yourself? The world is going to tell you that you need to lose weight, what you need to buy and wear, how your hair should be, what the challenge of the week is, what car you're supposed to drive, how you're supposed to live, what a perfect family looks like, and so on. Would it be healthy to be the one person to tell you that you're pretty dope regardless?

In hindsight, from the most minute thoughts of self-depreciation all the way up to some of my worst decisions thus far, I can't help but snap out of it and remind myself that life is too short for that. When a negative thought creeps in, or when you're about to make a poor decision, I want you to snap out of it and say this out loud: "Life is too short for that." Clap with it. "Life is too short for that."

I know you want to go off on him. I know she deserves a clap back. I know you want to snatch up that one colleague. I know you want to feel bad about your situation, but life is too short for that.

I'm convinced that one of the worst mistakes we can make in life is to think that we have time. I mean, we kind of have time because we have hopes for tomorrow, but we really don't have time to waste because tomorrow isn't promised. Life is too short to waste your energy and thoughts on things that don't matter. I'm going to be giving you some unfiltered truth up in here. I hope you don't mind fast-forwarding to being real friends because that's what I'm going to give to you. Wake up, Fren! Please stop wasting time!

We've spent enough time harboring over the past, rehearsing those bad moments in our minds, feeling sorry for ourselves, beating on dead relationships, keeping fake friends, looking at likes and followers, accepting passive-aggressive behavior, being surrounded by echo chambers and "I agree with you" people so much that it makes it hard ... to just silence the noise and focus on you. If it's OK with you, I'd like to be the not sugarcoated, *not really here to spare your feelings yet I love you* friend. In this moment, I need you to stop wasting the life you have, to stop being soft and in your feelings, to stop wasting time feeling sorry for yourself throughout this journey, and to stop making excuses. Out of that estimated one hundred million sperm count that was in that one buss ... you pushed through to get here. You! It's time to stop playing with your potential.

I'm going to do my best at sharing how I moved past a few hurdles, and by doing that, I want you to know that your past does not define you. Even if you failed five minutes ago. That moment does not define you. You are in total control of your feelings, and you get to decide what you want to do with them. I hope you choose to use your feelings to empower you so that others can be empowered. Another person's breakthrough is on the other side of your breakthrough. Chain breaking is a domino effect.

I want to take a moment to talk to the person who is stressed. The person who feels stuck. The person who wants to quit their job, the person who is tired of dating, the person who is tired of being overweight—whatever it is. I'm talking to those of you who are sick and tired of being sick and tired. The person who doesn't think that they are capable or deserving of whatever they want to pursue and who hasn't been able to find the time or courage to execute. I'm talking to you. Be it a new business, a new job, a new, healthy relationship, a body goal, another baby—whatever it is, your first assignment is to empty yourself. You're carrying way too much.

Let me walk you through what emptying yourself looks like for me. It may not look like this for you, but this is what it looks like for me. Starting completely over, from scratch, mentally. It's not pretty reframing your mindset, and that reframing is ongoing. If you're one of those people who cry superficial tears, are afraid to have hard conversations, or are afraid to stand in your closet and yell at the top of your lungs at absolutely nothing, this section is not for you.

This section is step-by-step training for your mind, spirit, and body to come into alignment in order for you to take walking in your purpose to a whole new level. If you truly want a breakthrough, I'm about to walk you through doing some strange thangs for a piece-a change. Not coins, friend. The change you want to see when you look in the mirror. After writing my last book, *Dash*, I made a promise to myself to write the book that people need to read. With that being said, let's dive in. Step one. Empty yourself.

MY POT

I wrote a letter for you. A letter you'll never read. A letter I wish would be important to you, but then again, I don't know what's important to you. All I know is that you've never showed up for what's important to me. For some reason, I thought maybe if I do things that matter, then maybe you'd show up. Not one but two graduations. Walking me down the aisle. The birth of your two grandkids. Those moments were important to me. I wish they were important to you.

As a kid, I remember waiting around for you for hours and sometimes days while you were out blowing the money we needed to eat. To eat. Knowing that you'd rather be away from your family, getting high, leaving us with the aftermath of your nothing contributions, which left me feeling like I wasn't worth much. It's taken years to see my worth. To this day, it's hard for me to process success because the lingering feeling of abandonment teaches you that no matter what you do, what you do doesn't matter. I spent a lot of time talking to God about fixing you, but instead, he's been fixing me.

Indirectly, I learned how to harden my heart and to only minimally feel the pain of people when they come and go. I learned that I'm going to be disappointed by people and that it's just a matter of time before disappointment sets in. I learned to make the most of every moment because you never know when happiness is preparing to leave. I subconsciously learned how to live in the constant unknown. We never knew when you were coming back or if you'd be coming back at all. We didn't know if the person on the other side of the telephone would be calling in request to identify your body or if the person ringing the doorbell was dropping by to offer condolences. We didn't know. As a child, I'd cringe at the sound of the garage door being lifted. That sound still haunts me to this day. Back then, my heart would race because I didn't know if your return home would lead to a fight with mom, which would set off my brother, which would leave me stuck, helpless, crying, and yelling as loud as I could for everybody to just stop—unheard, shaking, and trying to breathe. Like, bro ... we didn't know! Sometimes the sound of that garage lifting meant that you'd chosen us this time. That we'd have you until the next payday. Weeks like those gave me hope that maybe one day you'd fully choose us. That sound, the garage ... That's what I hear when my husband comes home every day now. The sound of that garage now means he's choosing us. His family. What I wish you would have done that. Can you imagine being triggered by the sound of a garage door being lifted? Do you know how often that happens? That sound is loud for me. Either way, with everything you directly or indirectly taught me, I learned that I'm in control of nothing outside of what I can control, and for that, I'm grateful.

Learning how to live in dysfunction at an early age prepared me for the curveballs life brings—whether it's waiting to be dated, the ending of friendships, businesses that I've tried that didn't make any money, unexpected death of loved ones, childbirth complications, being diagnosed and misdiagnosed with a skin disorder, more than twenty-two surgeries by doctors trying to figure it out, going through substance abuse myself, self-abuse, marital stress, parental stress, self-confidence shifts, questioning God, the instant stop of a new normal like COVID-19, and the daily unknowns of living while Black. Everything crazy that life brings was taught to me through God allowing me to have this upbringing. It's because of you that I've gotten the chance to learn that the pain we get to experience prepares us for what's coming in the future. Having you as a father prepared me for every level of disappointment. Your parenting taught me to be fearless. As an adult, I choose not to look at pain as something that I have to go through. I look at pain as something that I *get* to go through and grow through. Pain has taught me how to build muscle, how to expect the unexpected, and it's the pain of life's experiences that has shaped my character.

I want you to think about what pains you. I wrote that letter to my dad. My dad and the life he chose are part of the pain I get to empty. To this day, I still get triggered. You may have a laundry list of things that have pained you along the way, but I want you to zone in on one, just one pain. Was it something that someone said or did to you? Is it something that you feel like you didn't have? Did someone make you feel some type of way about yourself? Whatever it is, I want you to write it down. I'm challenging you to put it on paper in order to make it real. I want you to write it all out so you can cry it all out while you write. I want you to read it out loud when you're done. I want you to scream, yell, and break down as needed. Sometimes when I'm emptying myself in regard to my daddy issues, I end up yelling things like "Why couldn't you just choose us?" I felt the passion of the Fresh Prince of Bellaire when he did it. That scene was real.

Before I turned my pain into purpose, I put up walls to protect myself. Do you do that too? It's OK if you do. I still do by nature. For years, behind the walls that I put up, I numbed my feelings with drugs and alcohol, stayed within the same circle of people who made me feel comfortable, talked crazy to anyone who didn't fit that narrative, and pushed the pain down as far as possible so that I didn't have to deal with my feelings. I leaned on drugs, alcohol, sex, horoscopes, unhealthy relationships, and excuses to cope. Just like him. As an adult, I realized that growing up with my dad halfway in my life left me feeling like I wasn't enough. I didn't realize it while growing up, but those feelings opened doors to me feeling left out, falling in with broken crowds who were like me, and not knowing who I was as a young adult. Does this sound like someone you know?

Practicing to expect the unexpected and running toward chaos helped me develop a level of peace. Oftentimes, my friends and family tell me that they don't know how I juggle it all, but I grew up in chaos. Chaos is where I live. Chaos is me. I am controlled chaos. For the most part, it's good chaos now, but throw a wrench in it, and it's on!

I did a speaking engagement a few years back, and I used a story from the Bible found in Luke. You know, the one where Jesus was asleep on the boat in the middle of a storm while everybody else was losing it? I asked the people in the room to share what position they embody during that story, and I want you to do the same. Go check it out. It's Luke 8:22–25. Pause and go read that before proceeding.

Are you chill Jesus wondering why everybody is tripping in the storm? Are you one of the disciples, stressed out and bothered by the storm? Are you the boat carrying everybody? Are you the person who's not even on the boat, not knowing that there's a storm somewhere? Where are you in the story?

Me? I am the storm. The way, my energy is set up. I'm either going to rock your boat, making you feel really uncomfortable and irritating your demons, or you're going to be at peace when you encounter me because you have the peace of Jesus. I need Jesus to calm me. Are you a storm too? Where are my storms at? From the front to back? Are you feeling that? Well, put your hands up and say, "Me too!" It's we storms with these crazy backgrounds and breakthroughs that are going to help change the world. The world needs us! And the crazies of this world are going to chase us! Those chasers are our people. Let's be storms together!

The biggest difference from the dysfunction I experienced growing up and what I get to go through today is that I get to control the level of dysfunction I create. Today, I wear the hats of being a wife, mom of two kids involved in extracurricular activities, supervisor at my full-time job, Houston Realtor, house flipper, entrepreneur, author, inspirational speaker, small business coach, social media blogger, daughter, and friend. I'm encouraging you to dream bigger and to step out and do what you dream about doing in order to create your own level of dysfunction, especially if you're one of those people who had a crazy childhood and today you're feeling like you're missing something. There's no way of getting around stress. Stress is inevitable. Good stress stretches you to become the person God called you to be. Therefore, we might as well choose to create the stress we want. For those of us who were brought up in dysfunction, we were placed in that environment for a reason, and we survived it. God knew you before you were in your mother's womb. Therefore, consider yourself planted there. In stress. The rest is creating the environment to thrive.

Growing up, what did your environment look like? Were you the oldest, leading your siblings? You may be called to be a leader. Were you an only child who got everything you wanted? You may be called to pour into others who did not get the love and attention you had. Did you grow up without a parent? Maybe you're called to be the reset button. What environment were you born into? There is purpose in what you could not control. Now that you, the seed, has blossomed, what does your plant look like? Are you thriving, or are you dry and brittle, friend? At the end of the day, we only have control over our own thoughts and what we choose to do with those thoughts. Think about what pains you so that we can continue to process together and address the seed of your foundation.

For the record, today, I'm thankful for the life I have gotten the chance to live thus far. It's because of my father that I get the chance to feel like it's my time to pour back into you. I finally feel as if I'm whole enough to help you mend some of the brokenness. I finally feel as if I am enough. I'm outspoken in my brokenness. I've embraced my flaws, and I'm in love with being a storm, although I know it is a blessing and a curse all at the same time. It's because of my Father and my father that I am perfect.

PLANTED

Do you know what your gift to the world is? If you don't know, what do you do naturally? What do people tell you that you're good at? Are you good at helping people? Are you good at supporting people? Are you naturally witty or funny? Are you usually the first one to take initiative? Are you a leader? Steve Harvey has a great speech about tapping into your gift, so I won't duplicate the wheel, but seriously, what's your gift to the world?

Mine is to inspire. I'm competitive and optimistic by nature. I can still remember a pageant my mom put me into when I was little. I had to be three or four years old. Knowing me today, you would think I strutted out on stage, smiled, and killed the camera, but it was quite the opposite. When it was my turn to walk down the aisle onto that stage, I froze! I stopped dead in my tracks, cried, and shook my until my mom graciously escorted me to stage left! I watched the other girls strut on stage like pageant naturals from my little corner, and I remember feeling like I wished I'd walked out there too. I didn't know it at the time, but that was regret setting in. Do you have a moment of regret? Something that you wish you would have done? I'm challenging you to go back to that feeling and to use that feeling to fuel your next opportunity. My mom never put me in another pageant, but she put me in dance, where I took that same feeling and showed out! I feel as if I've been repeating that same feeling my entire life. I'm not interested in missing an opportunity that I want to do. If not you, then who, Boo? Somebody else is going to get out there and strut like those other little girls. Watch the person who is doing what you want to do, borrow their confidence if you don't have your own, choose the lane that fits you (like my mom put me in dance), and you get out there and kill it! You don't have time. In the hope that you have time.

I also have a gift of looking at the bright side of things. I don't know if it's the Sagittarius in me or what, but to me, there's always a bright side. You have to empty yourself in order to see it. The same amount of energy that we use to think bad thoughts is the same amount of energy we use to think positive thoughts. I don't care if I eat two bags of my favorite candy (peanut M&Ms) back to back or if I clap back NOT in all caps. I give myself credit for the small things. I could've eaten three bags, or I could've responded in all caps with shots fired. No matter the situation, there's always a bright side. The flip side is that there is a dark side too. It's hard to see through the dark, and that's where most people live. In the dark side. If you know a complainer or a woe-is-me person, that's a dark sider! *Run!* If you don't run, you will become the next one. Read that again.

There's a story in the Bible where God healed a paralyzed man because he had friends who carried him to go meet Jesus. That's a lightbulb to remind you that who you associate with matters.

Consider the dark side as a person or habit that's blocking your vision. I included the example of a habit because sometimes the dark side is you. You don't have time for that! *We* don't have time to waste. Someone else is waiting on you to walk in your purpose so that they can get started walking in theirs. Remember ... it's a domino effect. I'm challenging you to be that one domino that starts the ripple. It starts with one. It starts with you.

It could be just me, but I've found that people who complain or those who are self-saboteurs typically have a whole lot of friends. Personally, I've found myself in circles where there's more than enough people to puff-puff pass to, and I've been in rooms where I swear it seemed like they were sitting around waiting to out-complain one another. Stop and listen to the conversations around you, friend. Are these conversations and circles pushing you toward your next level, or are those conversations about things that ultimately don't matter? I'm not judging anyone, but I can't tell you what's going on in anyone's life but my own. I don't know the Housewives, I don't know who killed who on the daytime stories, nor do I know what somebody posted unless they tag me. If you run into someone who has a negative outlook or is filled with excuses and complaints, run! If you are the person who has a negative outlook and you've been making excuses about where you are in life, sis ... *stop*!

Want to find out who your real friends are? Try being positive. Better yet, be positive and pursue your goals. That'll definitely weed them out. Most people have been stuck in the same season for so long. Most people aren't pushing to reach another level in life. By choosing to be positive and go for more, you're going to naturally grow out relationships that no longer fit the pot, unless they're growing too. Consider your gift as the seed God planted here on this earth. It's up to you to take action to work and place yourself in the right soil. Your soil is found in connecting with the right relationships. The right group of friends. The right career. The right business. No matter what, there's soil out there that you can grow in.

This book is soil. It's truly a gift designed to show you that you're not alone and that you're perfect too. The bond we're creating with all of you is the perfect setup for success. What you decide to do next will determine if you're going to walk through door number one of walking in your purpose or if you're going to stay on the other side of the door, where it may be a bit dark. I promise I'm going to keep talking to you until you decide to come on the other side of the door! It's going to get lonely while you're building, but consider what's at stake. You have to push. Your future is at stake. Your legacy is at stake. The highest level of you is waiting. Consider this as an opportunity to choose in between the blue or red pill from *The Matrix*. Are you ready to be woke, or do you want to stay asleep? There's only one way to get to the next level. There isn't more than one door. There's only one door built for you. Your path. Your lane. You have to open this one door in order to open the next door assigned to you within this path. This is your life. The only way to get to the next level of unlocking your purpose is to go through door number one. Insert your name here. That's the name of the door. If I were at your home right now, I'd ask you to go look in the mirror. Remember, it's you against you. No one else. Door number one of saying yes to the opportunity to go *beast mode* is presented right here before you. What have you thought about doing but still haven't done? Are you supposed to write a book? Are you supposed to change careers? Are you supposed to go back to school? Are you supposed to get out of that toxic relationship? Are you supposed to start that business? Is there someone you need to forgive? Is the someone you need to forgive yourself? What is stopping you from clarity and moving forward? Success isn't just what you produce on the outside. Success is also the hurdles you jump internally. Mastering forgiveness, sobriety, eating healthy, and so on breaks generational curses too! Follow these four steps and say yes to the curiosity that stings. Give yourself permission to go after the things you said you want on your vision board and quit playing. The clock is ticking.

WATER ME

"He creates each of us by Christ Jesus to join him in the work he does, the good work he has gotten ready for us to do, work we had better be doing" (Eph. 2:10 MSG).

My life changed when I discovered my purpose. I'd just turned thirty-one. I'd just given birth to my son. I can still remember that winter season as if it were yesterday. Every year for my birthday in December, I create a new vision board. I focus on what I want my life to look like for the following year, and then I browse through magazines to find and cut out pictures that model the image and feeling that I want to achieve. It's my birthday present to myself every year. This particular year was all about learning how to become a mother and losing weight. I was due to deliver in less than sixty days, so this vision board had images of fruits and vegetables, a woman holding her son, a family of three, and there was one image in particular that was a woman holding measuring tape around herself. That was when I realized that the woman on my vision board jogged a memory of a flyer I'd picked up four or five months prior to cutting out that image. I got up from the floor with cramped legs from sitting Indian style for too long. I ran upstairs, dug through my old purse, and there it was. It was the same woman on my vision board.

I know you're reading this on pins and needles, waiting for me to get to the point, because you, too, want to discover your purpose. I'm intentionally walking you through step by step as to what happened to me. I want you to grab a pen and piece of paper so that you can take a few notes while I finish up this piece of my story. Your purpose is probably staring you right in the face, and I don't want you to miss it. Just in case you missed it, step one is creating a vision board. Write that down as step one.

After I realized that the woman on my vision board was the same woman on the flyer, I picked up the phone and scheduled a consultation. A few days later, the woman came over to my house. She measured my waist with measuring tape just like the picture, and she applied a product to my stomach area just as previously discussed. While we sat there waiting on the results of the product, she shared the story as to how she became a consultant herself. As she talked, I played with my then-four-week-old son. I tuned out most if not all of what she was saying until I heard her ask me if I wanted to start my own business too. I told her no. My personality has always been very direct and to the point. Her face changed from excitement to understanding while I showered her with reasons to support my answer. I shared how I'd just given birth, I was preparing to return to work, my husband and I already had a business, and I just didn't have time. On the way to escorting her out the door, she said something that has since stuck with me. She said to me, "Deidra, busy people stay busy. I hope you at least think about it."

Fast-forward from that moment in March 2013 to today, and I can't even begin to count the number of doors that have opened up. Her words fell true. Busy people do stay busy. Since then, God has opened countless doors for me. Some of the doors include but are not limited to building a five-figure-a-month business online, writing and marketing an Amazon Best Seller, promoting three times in two years occupationally, and being blessed to help thousands of people across the globe in building their own home-based businesses. Those doors then led to more doors, such as real estate, speaking engagements, and guest appearances on various podcasts and radio stations. Your next door starts with you saying yes.

If you've read my first book, *Dash*, and you still haven't discovered your purpose and gone to the next level, I'm encouraging you to go back, read *Dash* again, and apply the tools that were given. It was intentionally designed for you to read it for approximately ten minutes each day and to be done by the end of the week. Specific keys to discovering your purpose are in the story mentioned above and all throughout my last book. Take time to plan your life. Create your vision board and create a discipline board, outlining what could potentially throw you off of your focus. Read that again. Expect those images to come into fruition. Listen to the conversations around you that align with the blueprint you laid out for yourself. Take action when you see the puzzle pieces coming together. Say yes! The signs are all there. Put this book down and write down the steps I just shared. Once you're done, pick this book back up so that we can get back to work.

BURIED

One of the questions that I get asked most often is "How do you stay so motivated, and how do you have time to be a wife, mom, entrepreneur, and Realtor, stay fit, keep a clean house, maintain a healthy relationship with God, have friends, post on social media, and work a full-time job?" The short answer is I'm not always motivated, and I choose to make time for the things that are important to me. Because I know my purpose, the vision for my life, I'm inspired to wake up each day to do better than I did the day before. My purpose is the fuel to my motivation. When you keep your vision board in front of you, it's easier to see what to say no to. I love happy hours, taking naps, and eating French fries, but if what I want to do doesn't fit the image I place on that board, I can't do it. Mastering and becoming the next version of yourself is discipline at its best. Trust me. I fall off more than I'd like to, but the board is there to put me back in alignment.

Think of step one like Siri. It's the road map to your own version of success. When you make a wrong turn, because you will, you'll know exactly where to pick back up from where you left.

What do you want to accomplish in the next year? Where do you see yourself five years from now? What does life look like ten years from now? If you cannot answer these questions, I guarantee you will basically be in the same spot you're in right now. I'm encouraging you to get clarity, and you don't have to wait until your birthday like me. You can start today. Lay out what you want to accomplish without the influence of anyone or anything else. Identify your own path. Vision boarding creates tunnel vision when you're focused. When doing your board, I encourage you to make sure that the list you make for yourself is realistic and attainable by asking yourself if you're willing to put in the work in order to obtain the image you paste before yourself. How do you measure if it's realistic or not? I'm glad you asked! Ask yourself how many hours a day it will take in order to reach this goal. How many days a week do you need to put in that amount of hours? Set the deadline for the goal. Does it match up? If not, it's not realistic, and you'll need to adjust the time and amount. Let me give you an example.

While writing this book, I have several other plates that I'm spinning. I have an amazing husband that I need to be a good wife to; I have two awesome kids that I need to be a patient mother to; I cook, clean, take care of my health, and work a full-time job eight hours a day; I'm in the middle of juggling four real estate deals; and I'm also studying for my real estate recertification exams. There are five tests. *Stressed* is an understatement. I need to complete ninety-eight hours of studying, and I need to pass all five tests in order to stay certified. I don't have much time throughout the day, so I broke my five tests and ninety-eight hours of studying down by setting a three-month goal. Because I don't have much time, setting one hour a day for ninety days was realistic for me. In setting this ninety-day goal, I even pushed myself to be held accountable at least eight of the ninety days to do more than an hour. The results aren't going to magically appear. Results happen by setting realistic, attainable goals that you're willing to work for, consistently, until the goal is accomplished.

The craziest part about being able to coach people, doing speaking engagements, and hosting level-up boot camps is that there are so many people who have this step mastered yet are still stuck in the same place they've been in years prior. The reason for being stuck is always the same. You have got to take action. Goals are about baby steps. It's the steps you take daily that add up to the big vision. The more consistent you are, the sooner your vision comes to pass.

Do you remember my story from earlier? How I ran upstairs, in pain from sitting Indian style for too long? How I looked for the flyer and picked up the phone to schedule an appointment? Symbolically speaking, this is action step after action step. So many of you posted on social media for a month and didn't get the turnout and support you were looking for, so you quit. Honey, posting on social media alone might be equivalent to just sitting Indian style. You still have to run up the stairs, dig in the purse, make the phone call to schedule the appointment, and more. Is this making sense? Creating strategic action steps separates the girls from the women. Anybody can create a vision board and post a few times. It's the action steps that are holding you back, and I'm here to help. I've got your back.

But before I drop the blueprint, where are my prayer warriors? Hey, girl, hey! Praying is the easy part. It's the waiting that you are going to have to make peace with. Having patience is hard. If you do the math from my story, clarity hit in December while I was pregnant, and the appointment didn't happen until my son was four weeks old. Waiting on God to show you what He wants you to do can be tiring, but if you know Him the way that I do, you know that His timing is perfect. I gave birth to my son during a waiting period. I learned how to take care of an infant during my waiting period. I became a mother during my waiting period. The waiting period is filled with fruit and frustration.

I call the waiting period the wilderness. The wilderness is that chapter of life where you know what you want to do, but there's so much going on in life that you just can't seem to fit in anything other than what life is already delivering to you. The wilderness can also look comfortable. It sounds like "money can't buy me happiness" and "that's just too much work." Trust me. I get it. I've been there. And those two examples are true. Money can't buy happiness, but personally, I'd rather cry in a Lamborghini than in a Cavalier. I'm not talking down on anybody. I drove two Cavaliers. But seriously. Think about it! Do you want to cry about being broke and nobody supporting your business or idea, or do you want to cry about being stressed out and not knowing how you're going to help all of your clients? Relationally speaking, do you want to cry about running the risk of them breaking your heart again, or do you want to fall back, fall in love with yourself again, and cry about being lonely? All of these are examples of being in the wilderness. Wilderness is transition. Wilderness is waiting. Wilderness is making excuses and making rationalizations to fit comfortability when you know deep down inside there's more to life than just paying bills, drinking on the weekends, and feeling lit when that income tax check hits. Are peace and freedom the goal or not? No scenario will be absent of tears. If you're reading this and are in the wilderness right now, it's all good. Someone once said that everyone is always coming out of a growth season, they're in the middle of one, or they're getting ready to walk into one. This book is going to help you get through all three levels of continuous growth.

To recap, we've emptied ourselves. If you've been following the title of each section, emptying yourself is preparation as if you are about to plant a new harvest. We've either cried, yelled, or written the pain out of our system. We've turned our pain into purpose through sprouting. We've identified that that pain was set up to set us up for success, and we've identified how to use pain as footstools to see past that pain.

We've spent some alone time to zone in on what we want to accomplish. We've learned how to put those short- and long-term goals onto a vision board, and we've identified how to set a realistic time line in order to get those goals accomplished. We've eliminated the known. Tears are coming, but we've learned that we get to choose what kind of tears we get to cry. We've taken control over knowing what stage we're in, and we've jumped ahead of the game because we know what's coming. Remember, we're either in a growth season, also known as the wilderness, we just stepped out of one, or we're headed into one.

I wish I could tell you that mastering these steps is what's going to take you from good to great, but this is just the beginning. Will this help you lay out the best foundation to build onto? Absolutely! You're not going to get that win on the outside until you get that win within. Unlocking the next level is internal work. I call myself levels for a reason. Success is like peeling an onion. There are so many layers to you, friend. There are so many ideas and so much wealth inside of you, and the world needs you. All of what we just covered is the warmup. Now let's get to work!

VISIBLE

"What no eye has seen, what no ear has heard, and what no human mind has conceived- the things God has prepared for those who love Him" (1 Corinthians 2:9).

I promised myself that I wouldn't drop another book until I was earning at least six figures. Not only did setting that goal help to create focus for my next goal, but it also helped me to set a standard of accountability for myself. In my first book, *Dash*, I mentioned the importance of having accountability partners and keeping your vision board in front of you. During this book, I want to dive in deeper on some keys to success in order to help you take action on what you said you want to do.

I attribute so much of my current level of success to social media. I have literally built all of my businesses there. To some, it may look like I post all of the time, but the inside scoop to marketing yourself is to go where the people are. If you're an aspiring entrepreneur, author, blogger, podcaster, artist, filmmaker, or Realtor, you should be using social media to market yourself.

Take notice that I didn't say to use social media to market your product. There's a big difference. No one wants to be sold to. Posting your product or telling people to buy your book is just as annoying as the people in the middle of the mall who ask you to come over to their booth. There is a strategy to getting people to ask you for your product and service. Are you ready to learn how to make people come to you rather than you chasing other people?

I'm in year eight of using social media as a tool, and rule number one is not to push your product onto people. People buy from who they know, who they like, and who they trust. The best way to promote your product is for you to become the product.

When I first started selling health and wellness products, I had it all wrong. I posted my product along with the price. I was a mess. I gave out so much information that left no room for people to ask me questions. I studied hours upon hours and read books upon books on how to grow a direct sales business online, and the best piece of advice that I picked up along the way was to become a product of my product. If you're in the direct sales business, use the product for yourself and share a picture of the results. This turns you into the product. From there, people will start to ask what you did in order to get the results. Do you see how you just turned the table from you stalking people to people stalking you?

By the time I started promoting my first book, I had learned the strategy of attraction marketing. I released *Dash: We Only Get One Shot at This* on the anniversary of my grandmother's death so that I could create a happier narrative for myself on that date. I was in year four of entrepreneurship when I released it. Again, I studied hours upon hours, and I read books upon books on how to successfully launch a book. The best piece of advice that I picked up along the way was to give away an excerpt in order to gauge interest. That strategy worked too! *Dash* turned into an Amazon Best Seller in less than twenty-four hours. I have no doubt that this book will do just as well if not better than the first, because I continue to be the product. Whatever that product is.

Some experts are going to tell you to create a separate page in order to promote your idea. I believe in working smart and not hard. This expert is telling you to do everything from one page. Your page is where the people are.

Share your story. Share how you got to where you are today. Even if you're on day one. If you were deciding to start sharing your story today, it would probably be a picture of you holding your vision board and sharing how you feel about completing it. The people assigned to you—meaning the people who are going to buy your product, read your book, listen to your music, eat your food, and so on—want to know you. They want to see your authentic self. The Bible is full of stories. Your story is just as valuable. Add new friends to your friends' list, show yourself as friendly, engage with the people who respond to your friend request, and share your journey. Your biggest supporters are people you don't even know yet.

Social media is an opportunity to build a platform to generate generational wealth if you allow it to. If you use it as a tool, you can build whatever you'd like. There are so many social media platforms to use. Pick your hammer. Pick your wrench. If you choose to use social media to build wealth, remember to consider and visualize every post as if you walked on stage. Your post is the public service announcement. Become a professional storyteller.

The last piece about being visible is to also take time for yourself. Having a presence on social media and then taking a step back still makes you visible. I get messages all the time asking where I'm at. The people assigned to you, whether to use your product or to keep up with your family, or if your gift is inspiration or motivation, falling off of the map is visible too. Please make sure to unplug and take care of yourself. Self-care is leading from the front.

DEEPLY ROOTED

I'm excited to bring the level-up workshops back. We held the first one in January 2017. It was called the Perfect Woman because I wanted to help every woman realize that they are already perfect but that they may be a little unbalanced. Each speaker focused on a specific topic from spiritual health, mental health, and physical health. Each woman shared a piece of their own journey and how they used that specific topic to help themselves and others. My topic focused on ensuring that all three of those pieces were in alignment so that you could then execute your ideas and trailblaze anything you put your hands to do. At those workshops, I share what to do, just as I am in this book, but go deeper into sharing how to execute each tip. Make sure to not only finish reading this book but to also attend our workshops so that your idea can be broken down into step-by-step action. If you want to not only be visible but also become deeply rooted in your purpose, in your brand, and in your ideas, you're going to need a mentor. I learned this the hard way.

I tried running my first business on my own. I thought I wanted to be a wedding planner. After coordinating six weddings on my own, I tapped out. It was too much work. I wasn't deeply rooted. Next I started doing radio. I thought I had content and topics that people would want to listen to, but it turned out people weren't committed to tuning in every Saturday morning at 9:00 a.m. It wasn't until I started running my health and wellness business that I planted myself and allowed myself to be mentored. I found leaders in my community who were making the income I wanted to earn, and I followed every step they took. I listened to their YouTube channels, I read every post, I purchased every book they wrote and read it, I listened to every LIVE, and I attended every meeting, conference call, and in-person conference they attended. I became a sponge. I soaked up every bit of knowledge they were willing to share, and soon, I became fluent in the dialogue they were exchanging with their audiences. From there, I started doing what they were doing. I became fluent in the industry. I would assume that immersing yourself in the community has to be similar to learning a foreign language. You've got to go all in! The strategy of immersing myself and following the footsteps of greats applies to real estate too. Success leaves clues. I dare you to humble yourself and allow everyone in the room to be stronger than you. Don't be intimidated by it. I guarantee that you will grow from that room, and I guarantee that most of the people in the room will want to share what they know with you. Ride the coattails of the leaders in your industry until you are able to make waves of your own. In addition to following the leaders in my industry for free, I also invested thousands of dollars into business, spiritual, and algorithm coaches who shared key steps to take in order to help me get to where I am today. Investing in yourself is priceless when you execute the action steps given. I'm challenging you to get deeply rooted into your industry and to find coaches like myself who fit the mold of modeling the direction that you want to go.

I MEAN ... DEEP-DEEP

It would be completely irresponsible of me to skip over another key element of becoming deeply rooted in your gift. That key is to determine why you're doing what you're doing in the first place. Because there will be hard days, and relying on your why will be critical to your success.

There will be days when you will not feel like working. There will be days when you feel too tired. There will be days when you feel like giving up. There will be days when you question why you had the audacity to even get started. On those days, remember your why.

My why is my family. I don't want my kids to want for anything. I want to be able to tell them no when they ask for something because I choose to say no rather than having to say no. My secondary reason is grandchildren. I'm a believer, and the Good Book says that I'm supposed to leave something for my children's children. I'm crazy enough to work hard and be the reset button within my family in order to leave wealth and real estate for my legacy. Why do you want that business? Why do you want that license? Why do you want that relationship? Why do you want to lose weight? Why are you writing that book?

When you know your why, you're able to give objection-busting feedback to every negative thought that creeps between your own two ears and to anyone who tries to talk you out of pursuing your goal. You will blow away like leaves on a tree when the wind blows hard if you don't allow yourself to become deeply rooted in your why. Reasons for *why not* are right there, waiting to play into a negative emotion, which is inevitable throughout building something amazing. Prepare yourself and get deeply rooted—I mean deep-deep into your why.

SUNLIGHT

Have you ever been a prisoner of your own thoughts? I'm the friend that my friends say has her life together, although it doesn't always feel like it.

Everyone tells me that I'm bold and fearless, but deep down inside, I still get nervous to put myself out there. I still get nervous before speaking in front of a large crowd and speaking up when it may make someone feel uncomfortable, but I'm just not crazy enough to be bound by that feeling. I'd rather let *what if* drive me rather than the feeling of regret. I'm unapologetic with that. If it works out, great! If not, oh well! Another opportunity is around the corner waiting. I'm not sure if my confidence is because I've failed enough not to care or if I really am fearless, but either way, the end goal is to just do it. You've got to put yourself out there and just jump. It's selfish not to. Someone is out there, waiting on you to use your gifts.

One of the things that I love about men is that they have a tendency to focus on themselves and to do what they want to do. Men, I'm not shading you. I wish more women would become more selfish and set aside time to go balls-out on what they want to do too.

Selfishness was never something that I was taught or practiced until my early thirties. You heard me. I want you to consider being a little bit more selfish. My grandmother was a single mom who sacrificed for her two children. My mother was a mom of two, married to an addict, who raised a family on a teacher's salary, and then there's me. By nature, I thought that my womanly to-do list consisted of taking care of everyone else and then using whatever time was left to do something for myself. God allowed me to learn how to nurture from their journey, but the habits and learned behaviors don't have to be obsolete. Watching that behavior inadvertently taught me to neglect myself and to put myself last. There are so many of you reading this who are doing the same thing. That isn't shade to our mothers and grandmothers; I'm just here to tell you that the opportunities are different now. Use what they taught you, and build on that. Before becoming a bit selfish, I did exactly what was modeled to me. I cooked and cleaned and was the maid, the chef, the Stepford wife, the teacher going over homework, the chauffeur, and more. I did all of those things but still felt unfulfilled.

In the midst of being burned out as a mom and wife, I allowed myself to learn how to be selfish. I was riding to Destin, Florida, for my birthday weekend with family when I read a line in Tony Evans's *Kingdom Woman* book that changed my life. "Men and women are created equal." Of course I knew that, but I'd never seen it like I'd seen it on that day. I determined on that day, since that is the case, men and women are created equal, why am I the one stressing myself out, worrying and working on the list of responsibilities that can be shared? So Deidra started getting her groove back. I began going back to the core of who I am before I started wearing all of the different hats that I get to wear. I tapped into the core of who I am so that I could go to the next level.

SUNRAYS

Deidra, at the core, the single layer, loves to laugh and have fun! I love being sexy and embracing the body I have or have not worked on. Y'all can get carbless and fit Deidra or fresh off of donuts Deidra, and I like me either way. I can be carbless in the daytime and be eating carbs at lunch if I feel like it. Who's going to check me, Boo? I like singing at the top of my lungs, on or off-key, and dancing like no one is watching. I like staring at the water, doing absolutely nothing other than letting my mind drift as deep as the body of water before my eyes. I'm challenging you to give yourself permission to fall in love with yourself.

Upon my return home, that line in Tony Evans's book stuck with me. I gave myself permission to not wake up every morning to fix breakfast, to lie in bed just a few minutes longer, to order takeout instead of cooking every day, to run out of juice and milk in the refrigerator. For years, I'd told myself that those things were my responsibilities, but they're not if we're truly created equally. I'm married, so this piece of the journey may not resonate with you, but this applies to the Boo too. Whoever that is. If you're truly single, consider this as being proactive. Talk to the person you're dating about developing a partnership in handling life. I hope having that conversation saves you some time.

When was the last time you tapped into the core of who you are? Once I learned to love myself, I began building on that.

BLOOM

I listened to a podcast somewhere along the way that talked about how Will Smith masters learning the last scene of the movie first. It mentioned how he learns the end first so that he can master the energy needed in order to carry himself through to the end of the movie. I heard that message and started applying it to my own life. The dope part about blooming is that you get the chance to push yourself and take baby steps toward your goals. The sad part about blooming is that not everybody will be happy that you're blooming.

I could write an entire book on the downside of blooming, but I'd rather give you the CliffsNotes version of how you may feel when your friends and family don't support you, when you make a win for yourself and your friends or family scroll right on by as if you never won, when people start to treat you differently because of your success. To whom much is given, much will be required. When this happens to you, I want you to remember that no one owes you anything. I want to encourage you to be your own biggest cheerleader. I want you to remember that you came into this world by yourself and you will leave by yourself. I want you to pay attention to the energy around you to truly feel if that person is pulling you up or down. I've had people who I love tell me that my business isn't going to work, that I post too much, that my products don't work, that they never received a product when I have receipts showing otherwise, and so on. I've had people I love stop answering my calls, tell me that I think I'm better than others, that I've changed and forgotten who I am. It's going to be a painful and lonely ride on your route to success. There are going to be several opportunities for you to throw in the towel. You're going to have to be built Ford tough in order to handle the negative energy coming your way. In football, players get hit the most when they're close to the end zone. If you feel like you're being hit with a lot of negativity, know that you're so close to a touchdown. More importantly, know that you have the ball. You get to call the plays. You're the one on offense. Jealousy, hate, and envy are real, but love is greater. Love yourself enough not to be moved by the criticism and hate, and love them enough to keep killing it right in front of them until they either level up or remove themselves. People who are on the same level as you or higher will congratulate you, send referrals, and want to stand next to you while you're blooming. Other bloomers are the ones who understand that there's too much wealth out here for anyone to be bothered by the blessings you are willing to partner with God on. Let the petty people keep playing around while you go drop God's flitter in their newsfeeds. Your happiness and self-love have to win in the end. Let me share a few ways that I like to help keep my mind focused on happiness and self-love.

PETALS I

I have a morning routine that is about to bless your entire soul. Do you already have a morning routine? All successful people have one, and I don't mean hit the snooze button, roll out of bed, brush your teeth, and get ready for the day. I mean a morning routine to put you in alignment to crush anything that comes your way for the day. If you do not think you are successful right now, I want you to implement this for thirty straight days and tell me how much this changes your life.

First, I want you to set the clock one hour before you normally wake up. I want you to sit up in your bed on the first alarm without hitting the snooze button. In my head, I just heard rustling and envisioned half of the room standing up with one finger in the air for a Baptist exit, but I'm asking you to hold on for just a minute. I promise that I'm going somewhere with this. When you sit up in that bed on the first alarm without hitting snooze, one hour early, you literally just got your first win of the day. You lose every time you hit the snooze button. You set an appointment with yourself that you failed to show up for. Hitting the snooze button is subconsciously creating a habit for you to not bet on your own self. How can you expect other people to show up for you when you can't even show up for you? Sit up. Back against the headboard. Crown on. This first win is crucial.

The second win of the day is a ten-minute drill. You can set an alarm for this. I want you to meditate on the things that you are thankful for, and I want you to visualize how you want your day to go. How do you want to feel at the end of the day? I'm crazy, so I legit ask God, "What do you want me to do today?" and I listen for an answer. I choose to feel what seem to be the most simple things, like my toes, my fingertips, the weight of my eyelids, and so on. When was the last time you were still enough to feel your nail beds?

We all have so much to be thankful for, and we take so much for granted. Give yourself permission to ease into your day rather than hitting the ground running or failing to keep that appointment you set with yourself.

The next twenty minutes of my day involves reading. I keep a book right next to my bedside for this reason. Pick a self-help book or make a commitment to read from the Good Book. My friends and I studied the book of Proverbs together. Reading that book alone was at least a thirty-day series of focused reading. Do you see how we're easing into our day?

The next twenty minutes is audio focused. While you're listening to a podcast, this is the time to crawl out of bed, stretch, and start getting ready for the day. Once you really nail this morning routine, this is the time when you can do your cardio at the same time. I love listening to a good Eric Thomas, Les Brown, Sarah Jakes Roberts, or Terry Savelle Foy podcast. They all do a fantastic job of feeding the right amount of brain food to help me fill my tank for the day. The last ten minutes of your one-hour morning routine is brain dumping. Write down everything you need to get done for the day (that you didn't write down the night prior), and write down the takeaways from your readings and audio that you want to carry with you throughout the day. I keep a planner right next to my bed where I'm able to doodle all of my notes and thoughts.

Doing this routine will not be easy. You will want to go back to sleep. Sticking to a routine takes discipline—the discipline that you're going to need in order to reach your physical, mental, spiritual, and relational goals. Decide if what you want is truly important to you, and fill your tank with this morning routine. I look at each day like a tank of gas. You cannot drive from Houston to Atlanta on one tank of gas, but you can get from Houston to Louisiana on one tank of gas. Fill up your tank with healthy brain food from your readings, audio, and cardio you crush first thing in the morning. You literally move all facets of your mental health, spiritual health, and physical health onto the F side of the tank when you implement this. What you need to get done for the day is described as the tank of gas needed to get from Houston to Louisiana. Building a routine is a game of inches. Set yourself up to bloom. Your mindset determines your level of success for the day. This book is the perfect book to lay next to your nightstand for you to read each morning. I know it's going to take a while until you get into a routine, so I'm dropping a list of brain food bites to help you realign when the curveballs of life get thrown your way. Following is a freestyle list of thoughts to use on the days you wake up too late to fill up your tank.

SIXTY-FIVE EXPLOSIVE BRAIN FOOD BITES

1. I am my only limit. I can do anything I put my hands to do.
2. Today is my day. I can do all things through Christ who strengthens me.
3. One day or day one. I have the power to decide.
4. When I'm tired? I just rest. Quitting is not an option.
5. I cannot win if I do not play.
6. Hope is not a plan. I believe I can, and I will.
7. My words are my future. I speak life to myself.
8. It's not about a clock. It's about consistency.
9. I will not make myself small for anyone.
10. Life's rejection is God's redirection.
11. Failure is just fuel for growth.
12. My life is made up of two dates and a dash. Make the most of that dash.
13. Giving up on my goal because of one setback is like throwing away my phone because my battery died. Keep going.
14. Get over yourself.

15. The same boiling water that softens a potato can harden an egg. What matters is what I am made of.
16. There is no growth without struggle.
17. It's OK to not be OK. I just can't stay that way.
18. Nothing works unless I do.
19. Rediscover what excites me and do more of it.
20. Complaining slows down progress. Choose gratitude.
21. I will make my reasons bigger than my excuses.
22. The world is waiting on me to share my gift with them.
23. Reset. Refocus. Readjust. Restart. Repeat.
24. I will forgive other people for me. So that I can move on.
25. When I think about stopping, I think about why I started.
26. It will never be perfect. Make it work.
27. I will react to drama with no reaction.
28. I can't go back and change the beginning, but I can start where I am and change the ending.
29. No one is greater than me but God. She sits down to pee just like me.
30. I will not explain myself to people who only want to understand from their level of perception.
31. Some of them will be happy with me, and some will not. God bless them both.
32. The one who falls and gets up is stronger than the one who never fell at all.
33. My mind is sharp and my head is clear as I move toward my dreams today.
34. My past was a lesson, not a life sentence.
35. My best teacher is my last mistake.
36. Believe in yourself the same way you believed the lies that shaped your trauma.
37. If you want something you've never had, you have to be willing to do something you've never done.

38. If it costs you your peace, it's too expensive.
39. When life gets blurry, adjust your focus.
40. So much can happen in a year.
41. It's not who I am that holds me back. It's who I think I'm not.
42. I'm not weird. I'm a limited edition.
43. I don't have to be perfect to be great.
44. When things get harder, I get stronger.
45. I will be the somebody nobody thought I could be. In a great way.
46. Life is too short to carry pieces of yesterday into today.
47. If the plan doesn't work, change the plan. Not the goal.
48. If someone is dumb enough to walk away from me, I'm smart enough to let them go.
49. A year from now, everything I'm stressing about won't even matter.
50. I cannot heal my wounds when I'm too busy hiding them.
51. What a beautiful thing it is to be able to stand tall and say, "I fell apart, and I survived."
52. When I stumble? I'm just going to make it a part of the dance.
53. Don't waste words on people who deserve silence.
54. I will stop looking for happiness in the same place I lost it.
55. Life isn't about what I'm given. It's about what I create and conquer.
56. Be good to people, for no reason.
57. Sometimes, no matter how badly I want things to happen, all I can do is work and wait.
58. I will say what I mean, but I will not say it meanly.
59. Everything I do circles back around to me.
60. We don't see things as they are; we see things as we are.
61. Old ways won't open new doors.

62. The best view comes after the hardest climb.
63. Every day, I wake up thinking, *Today is going to be better than yesterday.*
64. The relationship you have with yourself sets the tone for every other relationship you have.
65. If I never fall, I won't know what a come up feels like.

Your mindset matters.

PETALS II: HE LOVES ME. HE LOVES ME NOT.

In August 2020, I got the chance to be a part of history. My family and I took a road trip down to attend the Martin Luther King Fifty-Seventh Anniversary March on Washington, DC. It was literally one of the top five most humbling experiences of my entire life thus far. I can still see the sea of people of all shades and walks of life sweating with masks on in support of the lives lost by systemic racism and police brutality. I'm feeling emotional writing about this piece of success because there are so many people who will understand my heart as I write this, yet there are so many who will want to pick what I'm about to say apart without wanting to understand what it is like to live a life while Black in America.

I'm *yella boned*. For those who don't know what that means, it means that I have a light shade of skin. I'm on the lighter shade of melanin. In the Black community, the shade of your skin is sometimes a conversation piece. Growing up, I gravitated toward people who were of a similar complexion, regardless of what race they fell under, because leaning too far left or too far right made me feel as if I did not belong. Our country is leaning in a direction where people are more open to talking about race, so I'm here to push a few buttons and help break some generational curses, now that I care less about leaning too far left or right. According to Ancestry.com, I'm bliggity Black, so technically, I can say whatever I want.

Being Black, at it's very start of Blackdom, has been painted as inferior to White people. Oftentimes, especially watching people who look just like me get killed for no reason at all, I think about why and how someone can hate us so much. I hate having to have conversations about death and murder with my kids. Life shouldn't be set up like this. As a result of subliminally being taught that we are inferior, subsequently, there is a slave-like mindset that is still prevalent in the Black community. I don't want to go too far in on my people, but, y'all … we have got to do better. Wanting cops to stop killing us is step one, and Black people doing better as culture, at least having a unified front, is number two for me. Can we please start complimenting one another instead of picking one another apart? Can we please find something healthy to say about the Black man and vice versa? Let's not forget that we have been taught to hate one another, that strong Black women don't need a man or partner, and that we need to spend money as soon as we get it. We were taught that. Stop it! When we do that, we're contributing to the division they want us to have.

Forgive your Black father for being too broken to be a part of your life or for passing down his brokenness to you. Forgive your Black mother for being too broken to love herself, which trickled over to you. Forgive the people who hate on you while you break the chains of times past. Forgive these people and move on. Time is not going to heal shattered pieces of our being, but addressing these wounds head-on will. Our culture is built on levels of brokenness, whereas we could be the first generation to raise children who don't have to heal from their childhoods, if we allow it. You can be anything you want to be. We have opportunities that our ancestors didn't. Heal, friend. You. Me. Us. We are dope, and it is time to start acting like it!

If you are reading this, you are here for a reason, and you have survived walking around for years in skin that some people still see as a weapon. Think about that. For years, we have been either slaves, oppressed, beaten, "freed," stolen from, killed, mocked, imprisoned, or dismantled from traditional familial systems, yet we're still here—considered a threat! How dope is that? The world order that we were raised in was set up to make us think that we are inferior to specifically White people, but how can that be if White culture continues to steal from us? Does a robber rob an empty house, or do the poor take what they want from the rich? Our music, our style, the curves of our freakin' bodies are being taken into doctors' offices so that they can be mimicked. You are the gift, sis! You've been quiet long enough. Shine already! Cues Beyonce's "Already," *Black Is King*.

Now ... someone somewhere is going to read this and not understand that telling my people how amazing they are is just that. I love everybody, but I'm about to single out the reader who may have found something of what I just said offensive by letting you know that you too are broken! Whoever taught you that you have to be a part of someone else's acknowledgment or recognition messed up. Butting in when your name is not being called is like saying "Here!" when the teacher called out Johnny's name during roll call. Please raise your hand and speak when your name is called upon. Please and thank you. Black Lives Matter.

If you are one of the people who are still afraid to look other people in the eye, are intimidated to have conversations of substance, particularly about race, or if you feel as if you have to change your voice at work, I want you to know that you're contributing to the division that is being highlighted today. I'm encouraging you to wear your hair. I'm encouraging you to be yourself. I'm encouraging you to embrace your own culture so that we can all enjoy the beauty that uniqueness brings. I'm encouraging you to move closer toward being respected rather than being accepted. You are an amazing blend of people who add flavor to everything that lands on your table. Don't you let these people or this world pick you apart, petal by petal, only to keep what they want from you while asking you to throw away pieces of you that are not acceptable to them. When you see me wearing a Buda dress, in bantu knots, jigging to Lil Webbie, I'll be leading from the front, embracing the skin I get to be. Let the people around you adjust to you for once. Embrace your grace.

BOUQUET

There are three other amazing women who will be sharing pieces of their journey in this book. Each of them were handpicked for such a time as this. When we first met up to talk about the idea of putting this piece of the workshop into written form, I thought about the *Women of Brewster's Place*. It's an oldie but goodie. If you haven't seen it, you need to check it out. In a nutshell, it's stories of several different women who end up on the same path and ultimately knock out the same goal when they work together. We had you in mind when we put this together. May your spiritual, mental, and physical health come into alignment so that you can achieve everything waiting for you with your name on it.

What was the last thing you specifically asked God for and then He gave it to you? I want you to keep that in the forefront of your mind as you take the next step into your journey. Your purpose is on the other side of the last gift God gave to you. I'll never forget when Gena turned to look at me and said, "Deidra, busy people stay busy. I hope you at least think about it." In that moment, I felt a millisecond of curiosity. Today, I know that the feeling that I felt was the planting of a seed. The stirring that you feel while reading this is no different. Ephesians 2:10 reads, "He creates each of us by Christ Jesus to join him in the work he does, the good work he has gotten ready for us to do, work we had better be doing." What are you going to do with that stir you have? Are you going to continue wasting time watching people live on Facebook, Instagram, and on television, or are you going to join Him in the work He does? The work He has prepared for you to do? The work you better be doing while you still have breath?

Your journey and your story matter.

PART 2
Genesis

I was *angry*. I was the angry Black woman. I later figured out I was the angry Black woman because I was an angry Black child. Why? Well, because no one addressed the trauma I endured as a girl. Not one adult in my life helped me process the pain I endured from abuse, grief, and self-loathing. If you are reading this book, I could be you, or you could be me. It's really that simple, because we all have experienced grief, dysfunction, and hurt. The good news is that I have relinquished the anger and replaced it with confidence, passion, love, and peace—all of which allow me to share healing tools with you in hopes that you can become the best version of yourself sooner rather than later. Today I am a successful psychotherapist, hip-hop artist, businesswoman, and activist. The journey to this perfect version of myself was a train wreck, to say the least.

THE ROOT

I'm an eighties baby raised by my mother, the epitome of a strong Black woman. It's important to acknowledge that understanding the story of your parents is essential to understanding the story of you. My mother was raised in a two-parent home until her ninth year of life, when her mother, the person she was closest to in the world, died tragically in a car accident. It's even more daunting that she begged, cried, and pleaded to go with her that day, as she did every time, but this particular day, her mother said no. I'm going to guess that no one, not one adult in her life, processed this pain and loss with her, as evidenced by how difficult it is for her to even think about today. As the youngest of five siblings, she was quickly sent off to live with her aunts, while her father went on to marry another woman less than one year later. Coincidentally, she was also separated from all of her siblings, who chose to live with different family members. Obviously, my mother harbored extreme hurt and anger toward her father and was estranged from him until his death. I met him once or twice, but for the most part, I was down two grandparents before I even entered this world.

Since no one processed this very traumatic event with my mother, and needless to say therapy wasn't an option at this time, the family filled my mother's void with sparkly, nice things. She always brags about how she never wore the same thing twice to school and always had all the latest name brands and toys. The long-term effects of this coddling is that my mother became, for lack of a better word, a brat. She struggled through school, fighting peers and defying authority figures. She struggled with reading and writing, so her verbal communication skills were superior. She never developed a filter, however. She made it to the eleventh grade before getting pregnant at age sixteen and deciding to drop out after a teacher threatened to call her mother and her response was *"I am the mother."*

The story gets gray here, because I'm pretty sure my father was significantly older than my mother; doing the math, if she was sixteen or seventeen, he was twenty-four or twenty-five. Strangely, no one ever spoke about this apparent age difference because it was normal for the time period. The two actually married, as during this time, if you got someone pregnant, you surely had to marry them. The marriage was doomed from the start, as my parents are polar opposites. My mother is street-smart, ambitious, and a social butterfly, while my father was nearly a mute, lacked drive, and did not care to socialize with any humans, not even his own children. Nevertheless, these people decided to have two whole children together and managed to stay married for five years. During the fifth year, my mother realized that my father was not interested in doing anything but working at the plant, coming home, and sitting on the couch like Al Bundy. My mother had dreams and wanted more for her life; she was mortified at the thought of being stuck in a boring marriage. She warned my father that she would leave if things did not change, but he thought she was joking and dismissed her complaints. My mother had such strong conviction that she immediately packed up her things and left a financially stable home with no job and two young children. At the time, I could only have been one years old at the most, and my brother was four. She left, filed for a divorce, and never looked back. As a natural born hustler who likes sparkly, nice things, my mother applied for government assistance and worked two jobs while raising two kids. Now this is the part of her story that she tells all the time, so I think she is very proud of this, and to be honest, it was impressive. She married my stepfather not long after, however, and they have been together ever since. Bless his heart.

My biological father's life is mostly a mystery to me. I was around him as a child, but he never had any meaningful conversations with me or my brother. He lived with my grandmother, his mother, so I am now certain that was the only reason we saw him regularly. I could spend the entire spring break vacation at my grandmother's house and maybe have two conversations with my father, the extent of which was either food or television. My brother and I never really thought anything of it since that's all we knew. Around my twelfth or thirteenth year of life, my grandmother died suddenly (we will discuss this in great detail later). After the funeral, I may have seen my father a handful of times and then never spoke to him again until I entered my thirties. It wasn't from my mother's lack of trying, however; she insisted that he continue to have a relationship with us, but my socially challenged father would never follow through. Many people have a great struggle with absent parents, but I honestly felt nothing at all initially, because I simply did not feel like I really knew him. Also, I had an awesome stepfather who quickly and proudly took on the role, so I never felt that I missed out. This did not absolve me from having daddy issues, however, because our parents have such a great impact on us—dead or alive, present or absent, healthy or dysfunctional.

I quickly inherited my mother's "I don't need anyone" attitude and asserted that I did not care to have a relationship with my father. Just because you say something with conviction doesn't mean it's real. The truth is I really didn't care to have a relationship with my father, but I was offended and appalled that he did not care to have a relationship with me! I was smart, athletic, artistic, and easy on the eyes, so I couldn't fathom why any parent wouldn't be in a rush to claim me as their own. Instead of labeling this correctly as hurt, disappointment, and confusion, I did what any sensible person would do—got angry and drew a protective wall around myself. Years passed, and I became more and more infuriated at the fact that my very present grandmother and uncle were taken away abruptly, while my mute father lived on to completely ignore me.

As a sidenote, you should know that my father was brilliant and athletic. I acknowledge that I inherited many of my talents from his genes. One positive interaction I remember with him is watching episodes of *Jeopardy* and *Wheel of Fortune*. I remember being in awe of how many questions he got right with little effort. However, he always struggled financially and never recovered after losing that job at the plant. He never sought further education or job advancement either. He was always fine with doing the simplest, least social job. He never spoke of any friends but was very close to one particular person. This was the only person—a cousin—he would share a full conversation and laugh with. I remember this distinctly. No one, except my mother, who had no filter, spoke about the blatant awkwardness of my father. It was a special kind of baby daddy drama for her because she clearly did not understand his behavior and was frustrated by his lack of involvement. As a child, my mother even had to take my father to child support court. During that single-parent time before she remarried, my mother pleaded with my father for regular financial assistance. Once again, not believing that she was serious, he dismissed her pleas. My father showed up to court with a shrug and was thrown in jail for failure to pay child support. This devastated my grandmother.

When she was alive, I think my grandmother did not usher my father out of the door because she felt sorry for him. They excused his living with her because she was an epileptic and would have grand mal seizures, which required assistance at times. My grandmother was an all-around badass, however, so I think she would have been fine without him—or maybe they needed each other. Either way, when she passed, he eventually lost the apartment she lived in and had to move on. Another source of my anger and frustration with my father is that he just packed up all of her stuff and left my brother and me with nothing. No pictures, no memorabilia. Nothing. To this day, I have no clue where all my grandmother's artifacts from the fifties and sixties went. It was rumored that he gave everything to another family member close to her, but no one really knows or has shared that information with me.

Having lost contact with my father from my teens, twenties, and into my thirties, I honestly intended to never speak to or of him again. One day, I received a call from my father's second wife, whom he had married and divorced as well. I knew nothing of the woman, but she was very sweet. She told me she was able to find me through Google since I am listed as a psychotherapist. She identified herself and told me that I had a younger sister, which excited me because I only had two brothers. She went on to ask that I schedule a meeting with my father because he was recently diagnosed with cancer and wanted to meet with all of his kids. I'm still not convinced this was my father's idea, but at the time, I decided to go along with the idea.

A few days later, my brother and I met my father, sister, and her mother at a coffee shop in a neutral location. It was a very strange meeting, which was only curtailed by the excitement of how adorable and sweet my younger sister was. She was around fourteen at the time and was very quiet and shy. The scene was my mute father, quiet and shy sister, almost as mute brother, his ex-wife, who was very sweet, and me. The whole meeting was very anticlimactic and lasted about twenty minutes. I don't remember if I hugged my father; if I did, it wasn't a long embrace. We had small talk, discussed what we were all doing with our lives, and exchanged information with our new sister. We made plans to spend more time getting to know our sister but nothing really for my father. My brother never expressed his feelings and is honestly just as nonchalant as my father about the whole thing. My little sister and I hung out a few times and spoke on the phone. She had other siblings as well but was excited to have another sister who she thought was "cool." I really believe my sister's mother was more invested in the process of getting the family together than any of us were.

A few months later, we received a call that my father had to go to the hospital for emergency surgery. Although my father never drank or smoked, he developed cancer that eventually went to his throat. It should be noted that my grandmother was a horrible chain smoker, so he was certainly exposed to his share of tobacco. My mother, having particularly sour feelings about hospitals and surgeries, immediately went into worry mode, which completely confused me, as I thought she could not stand my father. She immediately arranged for me to meet her at the hospital to visit him, which was more for her than me. We went into the hospital room, where my father had tubes in him but was in normal blah spirits. He asked if I wanted to see his stitches from the surgery. Seriously, this is what he thought to say to me. I said sure, and he showed me, to which I responded, "Wow." My mother and father reminisced, with my mother doing most of the talking. The visit was about thirty minutes at best, and I waved goodbye, walking out of the door. My father passed away shortly after that. I was mostly numb after being told and certainly wasn't sure what I should feel. I hadn't seen my father in maybe twenty years; he died within six months of my reconnecting with him. I mostly felt sorry for my younger sister, who was devastated by his abrupt death.

The funeral was another strange event, as I did not know or remember most of the people who attended. They put my brother, sister, and me in the front row, which felt awkward to me because I did not feel that was where I belonged. They gave these heartfelt speeches about my father's character, which, now looking back, was the most information I ever received about him. According to these family members and friends, he had returned to the church and was even heavily involved, he spent time with family, including my sister and her siblings, and he worked as a janitor at the local university until his death. They claimed he had a good sense of humor and was very caring to everyone around him. This was clearly not the same person I experienced twenty years prior, and to be honest, I felt slighted by that. Not only was my father not present when he did make positive changes in his life, but he still did not see fit to include me or my brother. I wanted badly to be angry and annoyed with my father, but by this time, I was a therapist and understood that he likely felt shame and did not know how to reconcile the broken relationship. Sadly, the trauma and dysfunction I endured with my absent father paled in comparison to my present mother.

My mother was the queen of the castle. Simply put, she wore the pants in the house. She was very strict and maintained control over the house even though she was always out or working. It seemed like all we ever did was clean. Come home from school and clean. Wake up on the weekend and clean. By then, there were three siblings, but my little brother didn't have to do much because he was significantly younger. I still get pissed off today when I think about having to clean my mother's room and bathroom. It felt like I was the only kid in the world who had to do that! When my mother came home from work, we instantly got a verbal tongue lashing if the house was not clean or wasn't clean to her standards. My mother rarely cooked because she had my stepdad to assist with this. Otherwise, it was the nineties food that people find charming today—bologna sandwiches, noodles, Hamburger Helper, even spam. She did not attend games or school functions, except my middle school talent show because she wanted to nurture my possibility of stardom. My stepdad came to what he could and was very supportive of my athletics and school work. However, he and my mother worked long hours, so most of the time, I was the last kid picked up and rarely saw a supportive face in the audience.

I remember wanting badly to join the band in middle school as a saxophonist. Unfortunately, the answer was that we could not afford to get a saxophone. Looking back, I now know that there were other options, such as a rental, but my mom never seemed to go the extra mile for things that mattered to me. However, she would scrounge up whatever money we had for back-to-school shopping to get sparkly, nice things. As a result, I was the kid who had DKNY and Guess clothes but no school supplies. Boy, that really used to piss me off because I was a nerd and would have rather had what I needed for school work.

I never shared anything with my mother because she came off as either angry, abrasive, or annoyed. In fact, I did not tell my mother when my period started because I thought it was something I would get in trouble for. It went on for some time until she found some underwear with spots hidden in the laundry. I was about twelve years old, but clearly my mother never mentioned that this change in my body was going to happen. We didn't talk about anything of substance until after the fact—my period, sex, abuse, and so on. The one time I did share something with my mother, she blew it up to epic proportions. In middle school, apparently a very rough time in my life, I was being bullied by two older students. Fearing telling my mother, I held on to the information as long as I could. At this time, we were living part-time with my grandmother, as something happened that left my parents living temporarily with another family member. Don't ask me what that was because no one ever talked to me about anything important. Anyway, I would work very hard to avoid these girls who hated me because some guy liked me and not them. They harassed me and took bullying to new heights, catching my bus and following me home after school to jump me. I managed to escape that tragedy with the help of my grandmother, but of course we had to inform my mother, who went berserk. She went to the school, cursed everyone out, and threatened the children, but she wasn't done there. We then went to the local police station and attempted to press charges and file a restraining order. Embarrassed is an understatement for how I felt, but it should be noted that those girls were sweet as pie to me from that day forward.

My mother had a lot of anger. She was always cursing out a cashier, getting into it with strangers and friends, showing terrible road rage. I noticed early on that no one ever stood up to her, not even my stepdad. Bless his heart. Her anger made her powerful, but unfortunately, when you fear someone, it's hard to feel loved by them. I probably got a total of three whoopings because I was terrified of my mother. On the other hand, it made me a very sneaky individual. Worse than physical punishment was the verbal aggression she displayed. My mother was famous for hitting below the belt and saying or doing the thing that she knew would hurt you the most. Once, yes still in middle school, I came home with a hickey on my neck. Mom was too angry initially to address me, so she made my father whoop me, which he had never done and didn't ever want to. I guess the whooping wasn't good enough for her, so she came into my room and ripped down all the posters of my very favorite girl group, *SWV*. She knew I was obsessed with them and valued those posters over most other things in my life. Thinking about the incident still stings to this day. She knew how to cut deep in that way. Emotional and verbal abuse are often seen as collateral damage in situations of abuse; however, we now know that emotional or psychological abuse can often damage a person much worse than physical abuse. This is because the bruises and scars are internal, piercing deep into the psyche of the abused.

We haven't even touched on the fact that I felt heavily ignored by the adults in my life. Although I was considered the golden child—good grades, athletic, creative, and well mannered—I don't remember ever feeling celebrated by family members. On the contrary, teachers and coaches loved and praised me. I was placed in gifted and talented classes beginning in elementary school, and I was always picked for performances, projects, and special field trips. It's not to say that my efforts were not acknowledged by my mother, who jumped at the opportunity to brag about her children's accomplishments. In reflection, I can see that the adults in my life didn't think I needed any attention, as from the outside looking in, it appeared that I was doing well. I learned quickly that the easiest way to get attention was from boys, hence having a hickey on my neck when I was barely into middle school. Sadly, I was introduced to human sexuality at a very young age, not by choice.

Around age nine, while my parents worked long hours, we would take the bus to a relative's house, who would babysit us until my mother got off work. I hated going over to that house because the other kids, I guess they were like second cousins, were what we would call today "ratchet." My mother wasn't fully aware of this, or I doubt she would have let us stay. At first glance, the adult cousin seemed to be responsible and relatively normal. However, when my mother wasn't there, we had minimal supervision, which meant we were left to our devices. One day, one of my older cousins got the bright idea to play "house." Turns out it was just a ploy to touch me inappropriately and make me believe that I played some role in the deviance. You may be wondering if I knew to tell my mother. The answer is yes, but if you remember, my mother is an extreme overreactor. Plus, I believed and was told that I would get in trouble if I made an outcry. As luck would have it, after several incidents, the adult cousin walked in on my teenage cousins touching me with my pants down in the bathroom. The original perpetrator had enlisted his brother to assist one day when he was present. When the door opened, I was both terrified and relieved. I figured even if I did get a whooping, at least I wouldn't have to be abused anymore or go over to that ratchet house.

The adult cousin was very angry. She yelled at the boys and gave them a severe beating. I sat quietly and waited my turn. She did not yell at me, but to my surprise, she pleaded with me not to tell my mother. She promised that the abuse would stop but that it was not worth my mother getting upset about it. I agreed because really all I wanted was for this to be over. My brother and I got in the car that day and never said a word. I don't think he was even aware anyway. We stopped going to that house shortly after but likely because my mother started to realize it was ratchet, not because it was full of predators.

I wish that was the end of the abuse, but shockingly, that cousin continued to abuse me when his family came over to visit or whenever the opportunity presented itself. I still didn't have the guts to tell my mother because I did not want her to end up on prime-time news. Around age twelve, however, I finally built up enough courage to tell my cousin that he would never touch me again or it was going to be hell for him. I guess he finally received the message because he stopped. It was frustrating having to see him when I got to high school, however. He only went for a few months, but during that time, he would talk to me as if nothing had ever happened. He even gave me lunch money with the earnings from dice games in the hallway. I knew his life was probably a train wreck at that moment, and that helped me let go. Before ever taking an Intro to Psychology class, I understood that hurt people hurt people.

Nevertheless, it certainly affected my views on sex and relationships. There was no worry about waiting until marriage or finding the right person because sex was just an act to me—something you did when a person likes you or you like them. As such, I was thirteen or fourteen years old the first time I had sex consensually. As with many teenage girls, I was into older guys, so my first experience with puppy love was with a twenty-two-year-old man. We actually carried a relationship on and off for a couple of years until my mother found out and snapped. Long story short, he served several years in prison for statutory rape. The night my mom found out, she also snapped on me, and it was months before I saw the light of day again. When we did finally talk, I remember revealing to my mother the sexual abuse but strongly minimizing the extent. It seemed as if it was too much for her to process, so we never really addressed it. Because my mother had no clue how to process trauma, she did what was familiar; she pushed it deep down and moved forward with conviction. I did the same.

The impact my environment and upbringing had on my mental health started to show in my late teens. It was sheer will and determination that got me through high school and straight into college, where I was able to reinvent myself—or better yet, invent myself for the first time. Going off to college is still the greatest experience of my life, for better or worse. The freedom of choice, the ability to choose your village, the opportunity to learn about what you love and to have diverse and new experiences. It was also in college that I figured out I was angry and needed to heal.

My sophomore year, I quickly joined a sorority, due mostly to watching the film *School Daze* as a child and longing for the experience of sisterhood. Fortunately, I did receive this experience and so much more, learning how to conduct business and getting to be involved in community advocacy. However, the symptoms of my trauma began to reveal themselves in the form of anger and aggression. It seems that I was always getting into it with one person or another at parties, events, or on the yard. It's easy to fall into the pack mentality in a sorority as a way to justify your behavior. I rationalized it as protecting my *sorors* and standing up for what was right.

There were two significant events that occurred one semester that made me take a good look in the mirror. At one point, I absolutely loathed the football team at my school. They were typical jocks, and their sense of arrogance really bothered me. One day at a block party, a football player kept taunting my sorors, and before I knew it, I had charged through the crowd to smack him in the face. Mind you, I was only 5'4" and about a hundred pounds at the time. Thankfully, my very large fraternity brother was right behind me and snatched me up before I could land the punch. It wasn't until later after my rage subsided that I realized I could have been severely hurt and may have put others in harm's way. The second incident was my sorority sisters simply telling me that they weren't sure if they wanted to go to a party with me because they didn't feel like getting into a fight. I had to admit that I was at least part of the problem at that moment and began to do some soul searching.

It's funny to look back on because I now value love and peace more than anything in this world. So, without seeking revenge, receiving justice, or possibly ever hearing the words *I'm sorry* from someone who hurt you, how do you maintain your mental health?

Start by being brutally honest with yourself; therapeutically, we call it taking self-inventory. When no one else is looking, you can grab your laptop or journal and jot down what issues you recognize within yourself (e.g., anger, hurt, resentment, fear). You may think of it in terms of what you believe is keeping you from your true happy place. After identifying these issues, you should go a step further to identify the root cause of these feelings. Who or what is the source of your pain and discomfort? When I worked for a treatment program in the prison system, one of the first assignments for the offenders was answering honestly "Who am I, and why am I in treatment?" You will find that the why is often more important than the what in many situations.

If you find it difficult to identify your issues and the root causes, you can always ask someone you trust who will tell you the whole truth. I was devastated to hear that my friends limited contact with me due to my aggressive behavior, but it was some of the most important feedback I have ever received.

DIG DEEPER

After identifying your primary issues and the root causes, you can now begin working on healing the wounds created by your trauma. If this task seems too heavy, it's probably a good idea to find a therapist you can really connect with. While we are here, let me get on my soapbox about going to therapy. As a therapist, I am sometimes baffled about the length of time and the extent of trauma people have to experience before they will seek therapy. Many people go only to appease a partner or their parents, not because they recognized the importance of mental healing. It really drives home the fact that we just do not value our mental health as much as physical health. If you experienced an accident and broke an arm, you would drive to the nearest emergency room for treatment. Yet, if you were in an emotionally and verbally abusive relationship, it could be ages—if ever—before you sought mental health treatment. I liken it to walking around with open wounds. We value and prioritize wounds we can see but ignore or minimize internal scars. Many mental health professionals will make the argument that the mental scars are just as significant, if not more so, for the individual to address. Next time you think about ignoring your trauma, picture yourself walking around with several open bullet wounds. We know that wounds, physical or mental, do not heal without some form of treatment, and left untreated, they often become infected. Thanks for coming to my Ted Talk. I will now step down from my soapbox and continue.

If you are confident that you can do the work and would like to take the self-help approach, this is also dandy. In viewing exhibit A, you will see a flow chart illustrating one theory of how we become who we are, flaws and all. This is from the cognitive behavioral approach to therapy, which is the theory I mostly subscribe to. It asserts that our thoughts impact our feelings, which in turn impact our behaviors. Digging deeper into the theory, we also learn that our thinking stems from what we value and believe, which is typically developed throughout our childhood from our environment and upbringing. Take a moment to view the example and then use the chart to complete a few of your own.

As you will see in exhibit A, a person growing up in an

emotionally abusive home where they are told that they are worthless and unloved may grow up to be an adult who values the opinions of others. This can be dangerous, since they are likely to encounter more emotionally abusive partners, who may reinforce the belief that they are unlovable. The person may constantly seek validation from others who may take advantage of or intentionally harm them. Once they truly believe they are unlovable, their thinking will reflect this, meaning they will make assumptions from the actions of others. Any negative interaction will be viewed as confirmation that they are unlovable. This can lead to depression, low self-esteem, anxiety, and more. Even when a partner means well, the person may sabotage a positive relationship, making assumptions and engaging in self-defeating behaviors.

It must be noted, however, that this chart can reflect positive behaviors as well, such as resilience, assertive communication skills, and trustworthiness. The truth is we can all have the same experience that yields completely different outcomes.

Case and point: my older brother and I. While I grew up to be ambitious, goal oriented, outgoing, and with a desire to devour the world, my brother is quiet, shy, and a hermit who has no interest in contact with the outside world. At forty years old, he never went to college, has worked the same job in the same position since age eighteen, does not have a driver's license, and lived with my parents up until recently, by default, because they moved and said he could not come. So how are we such polar opposites?

There's this ongoing argument in the mental health world regarding nature versus nurture. Does who I become have more to do with my genetic makeup or the environment I am raised in? My brother and I have the same genes and the same upbringing, but our views of the world are very different. So, while my genes and environment were very integral in my journey, we must also account for certain innate qualities that shape our personalities. In therapy,

I sometimes tell clients that there are two types of people in this world: sinkers and swimmers. It can sound harsh, but really, if you look at it, there are certain people who, no matter what you throw at them—abuse, financial strain, disabilities—they will adjust and continue to swim. On the other hand, some people will allow each set back to pull them farther and farther away from shore. I want you to know that your view of the world around you has a very great impact on how you interact in it.

Environment   (Emotionally abusive upbringing)

Values   (The opinions of others)

Beliefs   (I am ugly and unlovable)

Thoughts   (Of course he didn't call back; I'm unlovable)

Feelings   (Sadness, self-loathing)

Behaviors   (Sabotage relationships, critical of self)

Exhibit A   Cognitive Behavioral Approach

MIND OVER MATTER

As with exhibit A, we typically do not have control over how we are raised or the environment we grow up in. Our values and beliefs systems are created early on as a result. However, if we really want to have control or influence over situations in our life, the best place to begin is with our own thinking. A simple illustration of this is the weather. I live in Houston, Texas, where the ongoing joke is if you don't like the weather, wait fifteen minutes. Houstonians have learned to adjust to the rapidly changing climate, where it can be hot and sunny one moment and then raining cats and dogs the next. We are resigned to the fact that we absolutely cannot control the weather, but we can certainly control how we respond to it. In the back seat of my car is a jacket, umbrella, and extra pair of sneakers just in case. If I wasn't prepared, I may be totally thrown off by extreme weather changes that would likely ruin my day. This could lead to unnecessary anxiety and frustration with unpredictable weather. So, while you're working on this chart, be sure to document all the negative thoughts that are influencing your experience of the world. Then stop it! Stop it by replacing the negative thought with a more positive or alternate thought. Then take notice of how different you feel and change your perspective to a beneficial one.

Now that you are aware that you may be causing a large percentage of your negative feelings, you can work toward focusing more energy on things that make you feel good. In my time as a psychotherapist, of all the hundreds or thousands of clients I have worked with, no matter the socioeconomic status or cultural background, people all seem to seek the same thing: love, peace, and happiness. As cliche as it sounds, it is the absolute truth, as people come to counseling for one reason or another, but it can always be traced back to one or all of the ideals. So, to save yourself time in the journey, go ahead and identify which of these you are really seeking.

THE OPTIMUM HUMAN EXPERIENCE

The next step is to actually take a different type of self-inventory. I love the word *self.* People have given the word *selfish* a negative connotation, which makes us believe it is not OK to be so. Be selfish. You cannot save someone else from drowning if you are sinking too. You must first learn to stay afloat before you can help others do the same. With that said, you must be mindful of the ways you need to take care of yourself in order to not just stay afloat but swim with confidence. Taking care of the self requires a holistic approach: addressing the mind, body, and spirit or soul. All too often, we tend to one part of ourselves and manage to neglect the other parts. If you want to have the optimum human experience, you must fully address all three parts.

Here is another opportunity for a moment of honesty. In exhibit B, you will find a simple illustration of a triangle demonstrating the connectedness of the mind, body, and spirit. We must be aware that the three parts are intertwined so much that neglecting one will almost certainly lead to symptoms in other areas. For example, when we feel extreme stress, we may think of this as a mental barrier, but most people will begin to experience physical symptoms, such as headaches, sleep problems, and appetite changes as the stress becomes more pronounced but not properly addressed.

Now let's take inventory on how you are doing in each of these areas. Think back to grade school, where we were assigned letters A through F to describe our performance in school. Using exhibit B, go ahead and assign yourself a grade for how you address each of these three concepts.

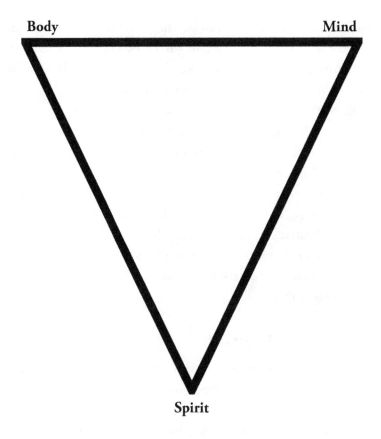

Exhibit B: The Whole Human

We spent some time talking about mental health but will also go into detail about physical and spiritual well-being. For now, note that taking care of your mental health means therapy, self-care, learning to create boundaries, and more. Physical health care is not just exercising; it's how you treat your body, period. Do you drink enough water? Do you smoke or drink? Do you address body aches and pains or just ignore them? Do you exercise but also find ways to relax and heal your muscles? There is a more holistic way of viewing self-care of the body. Finally, the spiritual aspect, which is often the most difficult part for some people. Have you found ways to connect to your higher power, and do you feel that your life has purpose? The spiritual part is not just about going to church or finding religion. You can have a spiritual experience through yoga, meditation, or nature walks. However, not addressing this part of the self in some way often leaves the person feeling empty and hopeless.

After you have graded all three areas and noted the ways in which you address them, take the average of the three for an overall grade. This, my friend, is the value of your current human experience. Seems like the average for my clients upon beginning therapy is a C or D-. The goal, in my opinion, is to work your way to a strong B, which is indicative of a well-balanced life.

If you didn't test so well, don't be alarmed. Knowing is half the battle. Now that you have the information, you just need to find the tools and apply them.

LET'S GET PHYSICAL

The human body, though necessary and exquisitely designed, is available to us for a limited time only. This means it's imperative that we take good care of it while we can. Unfortunately, many of us abuse or neglect our physical selves for one reason or another. We tend to allow life (work, school, relationships, etc.) to get in the way of our physical self-care. When people think about physical self-care, they automatically jump to exercising, maybe because the vanity in human beings is mostly concerned with looking good on the outside. I strongly believe that physical self-care starts on the inside, as do most things having to do with the human experience. Then again, I may just be saying this because working out is my least favorite thing to do!

One particular blessing from my gene pool is my petite frame, as I love to eat and despise exercising. I used to try to keep up with workout enthusiasts, lifting weights, running, and working with a personal trainer, but eventually I had to figure out what plan for physical self-care was most realistic for me. Physical health is important to me because I have lost many people to one disease or another and I would like to experience longevity. If I'm being honest, losing so many people at a young age can make you obsess over mortality and the realization that we are here for a limited time only. It does frustrate me when people I care about don't value their health or time on this earth, but I have to reconcile that their journey does not belong to me.

I also grew up in a house with a presumed hypochondriac, my mother. She would go to the doctor for everything and anything. She worked in the medical field, so she was always coming home with news of the latest disease or a tragic story about someone dying. I am sure her anxious energy eventually passed on to me. It definitely started in my early teens when I found a lump in my breast. My mother became frantic and immediately scheduled a doctor's visit. After running tests, the doctor revealed that the growth was benign and basically harmless. The doctor explained that I should stay away from chocolate and anything containing caffeine. Of course, they gave the option to remove the tumor because well … money. My mother had me scheduled for surgery by the next week. I remember being so terrified at thirteen years old by the idea of going under anesthesia and being cut open by a stranger. Now, as the ride or die she is, my mother was there when I went to sleep and the first face present when I woke up. I was happy to have made it through it but also bummed that I had an ugly scar on both breasts. The healing process was awkward but fine, and I was back up and running soon after—until the next year when we found more lumps. We did the tests again, and again they were benign. However, in true fashion, my mother scheduled another surgery, this time against my preference. By this time, the doctors were telling me that it was hormonal and they could completely go away by adulthood or when I became pregnant. It would have been my preference to wait it out and continue to get yearly checkups, but my opinion was not considered. So here I am today with three scars between both breasts and still another lump.

This story is important to talk about, as we have been discussing the medical treatment of Black women in the media. I want to share this story with anyone who doesn't know that they should absolutely advocate for themselves and must.

As I grew into adulthood, I became more interested in a holistic approach to medical treatment. It became clear to me that every year, the doctors could not wait to bill me for all the tests (e.g., mammogram, biopsy, x-ray, etc.) without ever offering real solutions other than cutting me open. After college, I joined a Tai Chi class, and it changed my life for the better. For those who are unfamiliar with Tai Chi, it is a Chinese form of martial arts that utilizes moving mediation techniques for healing. So it is exercise but also teaches you how to heal the body through simple movements. In addition, it also addresses the mind and spirit, which I loved. The first session was a consultation in which you meet one-on-one with an instructor who was very serious about the craft. They basically assessed me physically and could tell where I was struggling mentally and emotionally based on that. It was a very powerful interaction. While some exercises, such as lifting weights, actually increase tension in the body, Tai Chi is aimed at full relaxation. In doing so, we were taught how to mediate in a way that was more helpful to me. As a person with adult ADHD, it was very hard for me to sit still and keep my mind on one thing or on nothing at all. I still find this very difficult. With moving meditation, it really worked because I was able to focus on the movements while taking my mind off of daily stress. By the end of the class, I felt very relaxed yet energized. I would recommend having this experience at least once in your life. What's interesting is that you feel like you have taken a medication to relax but instead have given yourself a natural sedative through relaxation of your muscles. I can't say enough about this form of physical self-care because you can practice it at any level of physical capability. Anyway, honest to God, when I practiced this skill regularly for several months straight, the lumps in my breast went away. Was it the release of tension? Was it the self-healing aspect and really believing that I could? I don't know, but it worked. Since I have stopped Tai Chi due to moving, one lump has returned, but it has never again been as severe as it once was.

After I moved to a different side of town and found that there wasn't a Tai Chi spot in my area, I knew I had to find the nearest yoga studio. It is clear to me now that I like workouts that are relaxed, fun, and not reps centered. Yoga is amazing because you can get major results from simply holding a position. I know some yoga instructors who are cut and have never lifted a weight other than their own body. That is fascinating to me. Similarly, one of my older Tai Chi instructors could do the splits with ease, while I'm still over here struggling to reach my toes. Anyway, yoga was and still is a great tool for my physical self-care but also a great tool for stress management. I'm not going to lie to you and tell you that I am a professional yogi. I am not. However, I have learned to stretch myself further than I ever believed I could.

I started out relatively young, working with a man who was a diehard yogi. He was Indian, which, from my understanding, is where the art of yoga originated. He was very strict about the poses and did not allow me to slack. I remember he even laughed at us "silly Americans" at times when we struggled with what he considered a simple pose. He practiced Ashtanga yoga, which is a structured form of the art in which you do a distinct series of poses the same way, every time. You start to improve and can eventually do things like fold your legs behind your back or keep your balance firmly while holding your leg high in the air. After some time, you begin to notice your strength and endurance increasing just from holding these poses, but even more is what it does for your mental discipline. This class was probably my second favorite after Tai Chi. The benefits of both yoga and Tai Chi include flexibility, muscle strength, weight management, healthy circulation, joint health, improved sleep, stress management, and more.

Before we move on, I want to mention the cultural aspect of attending a yoga or Tai Chi class. Before you try these classes, I would do research on the organizations. As a woman of color, it is very unsettling for me to go to a yoga studio that consists of 99 percent bubbly White women trying to teach me about an ancient Indian practice. It just feels weird to me, so I guess it's a personal preference. The appropriation of cultural art forms is a big issue for me personally, so I choose to not occupy spaces that have this vibe. There are plenty of studios to choose from, and I have found several that have a diverse instructor roster. Whether you choose to go to a gym or studio, you should make sure you feel comfortable in that space, especially if you want to commit to the program long-term.

Another form of exercise I take great pleasure in doing is Zumba. I'm sure many of you have tried this type of class, due to it becoming popular in mainstream media over the last few years. Zumba is my jam because it is fun and carefree and incorporates my favorite genres of music. My favorite instructor to date was an openly gay Black man who wasn't afraid to make us twerk right after a salsa move. As much as I love to dance, I am not great at learning choreography on the spot. The good news is that it's pretty clear that most of the people in class don't know what the hell they are doing either, which makes it fun. Zumba is great for burning calories, boosting your heart rate, building endurance, destressing, and improving coordination. I also like that you can drop in on any class and jump in the choreographed sequence.

Other than these forms of exercise, I try to walk, jump rope, and follow along to YouTube exercise videos when I can't get to the gym or studio. One form I am looking to try is Pilates, as I've heard that the benefits are similar to yoga, with an emphasis on muscle strengthening and toning, which is what I desire most right now.

YOU ARE WHAT YOU EAT

You are what you eat. That's just what it is. Many of us will have a lifelong tumultuous relationship with food, knowing the things that taste the best often are the worst for us. Growing up in the dirty South with family from Texas, Louisiana, and Mississippi, soul food and Cajun food were always a part of my diet. I still to this day haven't met another person who can make seafood gumbo the way my grandmother did. The problem with these foods is not only the unhealthy ingredients but also the oversized portions that we consume. Not to mention, in my family, dessert after every meal was basically a requirement.

For many years, this did not faze me because I was thin and petite, so portion control was not on my mind. Then I hit those thirties, and the junk and soul food started to go straight to my thighs and stomach. Being a woman can be so challenging, as if we don't have enough obstacles to face, being expected to rear children, work, and save the world. At a certain age, our bodies begin to turn against us. At the time, I was happy though, because I finally felt like I had the figure of a woman and not a teenage girl. I love my hips, a gift from my grandmother, and overall, I am generally happy with my body because I have just never been a vain person. My struggle with food comes from finding out the horrors of the food industry. The magnitude of deception and negligence involved in the meat and fast-food industries astounds me. Like I said, longevity is important to me, so I can't see that happening by eating American food regularly.

As such, I went straight vegan for about five or six years. This was probably during the time of me doing Tai Chi as well, so it was a very health-conscious period in my life. Here's the thing: veganism is hard as hell for a southern Black woman. I essentially had to stay away from particular people, places, or things like an addict in recovery. Of course, I felt great and was a picture of health. It's definitely easier to be vegan or vegetarian when you have to be responsible for only one person. I cannot imagine trying to do this with an entire family, so I commend people who can do so. It was especially difficult for me, however, because I do not cook, nor do I enjoy cooking. This was also at a time when there were very few vegan restaurant options. Now they are plentiful.

On a vegan diet, you begin to understand that food is really supposed to be for replenishment of nutrients, not just to satisfy taste buds. The common saying is "eat to live; don't live to eat." When you approach food in that manner, the gluttony of it all becomes glaringly obvious. We really don't need half of the things we consume, but on some level, it makes us feel good. If you find yourself overeating or binging, it may be time to check the emotional and psychological connection you have with food. Let's face it. When we are stressed, depressed, and even bored, we tend to crave foods we want but may not need. Guess what? There is actually a scientific reason for this. At a very young age, we are taught to use food as a tool for comfort or a source for rewards. Think about parents who promise to buy their kids ice cream or their favorite snack when they accomplish a task, or offer a child candy to comfort them when they are sad. We essentially set up our children to associate feelings with food. So, while it is awesome to diet and exercise, once again, we must consider the entire person, even when it concerns food consumption. If you are finding yourself eating emotionally, to the point where it is disruptive in your life, it may be time to see a therapist to identify underlying issues associated with eating.

Back to my journey with food and dieting. Eventually, living in the South and trying to be a vegan just wasn't working for me, so I decided to transition to being a pescatarian. For those who may be unaware, a pescatarian does not consume meat products but will eat fish and other seafood. A basic description is that a pescatarian won't eat anything that walks on land. However, some pescatarians make an exception with eggs and dairy. When I joined the pescatarian lifestyle, I chose to consume eggs but still avoided dairy. This diet was much easier for me because I am an avid fan of seafood, including fish, crawfish, shrimp, and oysters. It really worked for my Cajun lifestyle. I must admit, however, that it did not give me the same health satisfaction that the vegan lifestyle did.

BE SMART

The beauty in life is that we have a right to choose and change our minds at any time. I'm sharing my food and diet journey with you so you can stop being so hard on yourself. No one is perfect; if we try and fail, we can live to fight another day. Many times, we just need to make adjustments and get back on the saddle. I think the most important thing is to be realistic about what you can and cannot do when it comes to diet and exercise. When I work with clients who have addictive or codependent personalities, it is always interesting to watch their struggle with quitting something. I can't tell you how many clients try to come in and say, "I quit smoking, cold turkey." It's only a matter of days or weeks before they return saying they relapsed. It's clear that people don't understand how habitual human beings are. If you don't believe me, pay attention to the way you put your pants on each day or even take a shower. Our bodies and minds like habits because they requires less thinking to complete tasks. So, with that cigarette, it's easy to stop when nothing is happening, but the moment a person feels stressed, the craving for the cigarette will return because they have already trained their mind that that is how they fix their stress and anxiety.

Therefore, if I want to change my behavior, I will need to replace it with a new one, taking the time to retrain my brain. The planning and preparation of this is the most important part of the process. In therapy, we typically teach people how to set and achieve goals by using the acronym SMART. This means that your goals should be specific, measurable, attainable, realistic, and time bound. In addition to this, however, I think it is also important to have a support system or at least an accountability party who will check in with you regularly and encourage your progress. Lastly, from my experience in coaching and therapy, when people perceive they have failed or relapsed, they may be more inclined to throw in the towel. With that said, I like to help my clients create a relapse-prevention plan and account for what they will do if relapse or failure occurs. Take some time to fill in exhibit C honestly and without prejudice. I also recommend finding a friend or two to go over the plan with, someone whose honest feedback you value.

Keep in mind that it is not a good idea to try to accomplish several goals at once. I would suggest prioritizing tasks by what is urgent, what is important, and what can wait until later. It's also a good idea sometimes to start with the simplest goal so that you can build confidence in small success.

Goal	Example: lose fifteen pounds.		
Specifics	Gym two to three times per week: lift weights / cardio.		
Measurable	Weigh in once a week, every Friday, one to two pounds per week.		
Attainable	Give ninety days.		
Realistic	Improve cardio and movement.		
Time Sensitive	Lose one to two pounds per week, ninety days target.		
Support/ Accountability	Best friend, partner; check in twice a week, work out with me once a week.		
Relapse- Prevention Plan	Allow two cheat days per month. If I miss a week, commit to an additional workout day. Call for support.		

Exhibit C: Realistic Goal Setting

While we are on the topic of physical self-care, I would like to give an honorable mention to a few other necessary behaviors I believe get overshadowed by diet and exercise:

1. *Get some rest.* When we do not get adequate sleep, we simply cannot function at the highest level. Even more importantly, lack of sleep can lead to physical ailments and mental health issues. People have been known to have psychotic episodes stemming from this; it's that serious. Show your body love by getting a good night's sleep or taking a short nap to replenish.

2. *Help your body heal.* When you feel sick, don't just lie around and hope it gets better. Take care of yourself by taking time off and addressing the symptoms. It's even better if you can practice preventive measures, such as taking vitamins and avoiding foods that increase likelihood of illness, such as dairy. In case you haven't been told, most diseases begin in the gut.

3. *Stretching.* This is such a simple activity that yields major results. Tension builds up in our body daily, which can lead to physical ailments such as headaches, backaches, and tightness. Stretching helps you maintain flexibility and decreases your chances of injury. It is also believed that stretching increases longevity and overall quality of life.

4. *Hygiene.* I like to include hygiene in physical self-care because looking good has a correlation to feeling good. Make sure to carve out time for physical self-care, such as hair, nails, and makeup. You should even address the parts you have been neglecting, such as getting a new pair of glasses or having your hearing checked. Go ahead and make that appointment for a massage. We could all use a spa day.

Overall, when it comes to physical self-care, please note that it's most important to do what's best and most realistic for you and your family. At the time of writing this chapter, I am standing firmly and proudly in my truth as a self-proclaimed 80/20 vegan. Basically, I have decided to dedicate most of my diet to vegan food while leaving 20 percent for the other things I love and simply cannot do without. After all, I live in Houston, Texas, one of the top places in the world to get delicious food. I try to make it to Zumba and hot yoga a few times per week while working very hard to get to bed at a decent time each day. I work to stay hydrated with alkaline water and swear by the elderberry. Luckily, I do not drink alcohol and never have. I know, but it's true. This is what is working for me currently and could change at any time, but as long as I feel good about the choices I'm making, that's all that matters.

FROM BODY TO SOUL

Full transparency, I saved the soul/spirit for last because it has been the greatest struggle for me due to trauma and some cognitive dissonance. My earliest memories with religion take me back to my lovely grandmother. She was a devout Catholic and took us every Sunday to her Catholic church. The most interesting part of this church was that it was predominately White. This was probably between the ages of five and nine, so they were likely the only interactions I had with White people outside of school. White churches are so different; at least that one was. There was singing, but it was very structured and more akin to a lullaby than a jam session. I remember the first time they told us to drink the blood of Jesus, or something like that, and eat a stale cracker. I thought it was cool that we got a snack in the middle of the program but also found it strange. We would always have to say ritualistic things like "the Father, the Son, and the Holy Spirit" and make lots of cross gestures over our body. With White Jesus plastered all around me, illustrating what Jesus went through to save us, we had to pull out a little bench, get on our knees, and pray. The whole thing seemed cultish to me at the time, but since I loved music, I managed to enjoy learning the songs. The statue of Jesus nailed to a cross is cemented in my mind. As eerie as I found the whole church experience, we were also greeted with kind words and hugs after, and then we got to play outside. I can't say that it was a negative experience because it seemed genuine and I completely trusted my grandmother's judgment of character. As I got older, I stopped volunteering to go to church with my grandmother. She never forced us to go but always kept an open invitation. She was so cool in that way, always providing us with diverse experiences but never forcing it down our throats.

She was very big on the Easter holiday, which now I understand was also a religious thing. My grandmother lived in housing projects but seemed to love it because she had direct access to the people in the community. She would organize a huge Easter egg hunt for the entire apartment complex. We would stay up all weekend dying real eggs and filling fake ones with candy. To this day, I don't know how she conjured up all the supplies because she never worked and lived off disability and my father's small contributions. Yet she managed to ensure an entire community of children and their parents could celebrate Easter Sunday.

As previously stated, my grandmother was disabled because she had epilepsy and constantly had grand mal seizures that were terrifying to me. One Easter Sunday, we had just finished hiding all the eggs for the other kids in the apartment complex. I looked up at my grandmother standing near the top of the stairs outside of one of the apartments. She began to sway as if she was about to faint, and as quick as lightning, she came tumbling down the stairs in front of me. I was mortified as my brother and I ran to assist her. My father came from our apartment to take her home, but she refused. They had to call an ambulance to check her out for any injuries, but she downplayed the whole event, explaining that it was just another seizure and she was fine. We somehow finished the Easter egg hunt that day and had a splendid time.

I now understand that my grandmother's spiritual connection was through the church, or some direct line, and my spiritual connection was through her. She never preached, and I never saw her use words in the Bible, which I'm sure she knew very well, to hurt others. Now that I think of it, she wasn't even prudish. She would curse and gamble and was very upfront about her shortcomings. It was through the actions of unconditional love, unwavering faith, and courage that we understood her religious beliefs. We can only aspire to be as authentic with our spirituality. When she died, in the way she died, a little of my faith died with her.

As tough as my grandmother was, the end of her life came abruptly and without significance. About a year or so before my grandmother's death, she did have a major accident during a grand mal seizure in which she dumped an entire pot of gumbo on her person. As a sidenote, the Cajun/creole/soul food my grandmother cooked was a spiritual experience that I have continued to chase until this very day.

Anyway, during a seizure episode, she dumped an entire pot of gumbo on herself and was rushed to the hospital. She suffered third-degree burns on one side of her body and had to get four of her fingers cut off because they could not be salvaged. As distraught as we all were, this lady found a way to make a joke about it. She would constantly make fun of her "nubbs" or use them to mess with us because it obviously freaked us out. It didn't stop her from doing any of the things she did before. She went right back in the kitchen to make another pot of gumbo. When people talk about the strength of Black women, I often wonder if they truly understand how resilient and determined they can be with even the most troubling of setbacks. I like to wear apparel that says the "Black Woman is God" because when I think of a higher power or spiritual being, nothing would be closer to that than a Black woman.

Alas, my grandmother died suddenly in her fifties, with so much more life to live. My mother called us to the room one day and said that my grandmother had been placed in the hospital due to severe abdominal pains. I remembered being at her house the previous weekend, and she was visibly in pain but never said it. I watched her double over in pain and spout out creole slang terms as she winced and rubbed her belly. Upon arrival at the hospital, we found out she was severely constipated and was in urgent need of an enema. I felt a sigh of relief when we were made to believe that the matter was under control. I have extreme anxiety regarding death and dying, which we will get to later, but it made me loathe hospitals. We came in to visit my grandmother for a few minutes. She wasn't her chipper, joking self and seemed more subdued. We had no idea how much pain or discomfort she was experiencing because she never told us. My mother, who was always on top of things, due to her own anxiety, spent some time questioning the doctors. I don't even remember where my father was at the time or what he was doing. We said our goodbyes, went home, and went to bed. The next morning, the phone rang, and my mother screamed, "Yvette and Roderick, get up! Grandma died!" Who screams out the death of a loved one to children? I remember going numb and into shock.

After the shock was pure unadulterated anger. I'm still not sure if I was angry with myself, my grandmother, God, or all three, but I am sure that I lost sight of my faith that day. The rage I felt was correlated to seeing my grandmother as the only person left in my life who truly understood and inspired me. The additional rage was knowing that my grandmother was an all-around badass but died suddenly and senselessly because a negligent doctor didn't perform an enema or whatever procedure she needed in an adequate amount of time. I was told that she died from bile backup, as crazy and random as it sounds. Having survived segregation, protests, epilepsy, poverty, third-degree burns, and losing an entire hand, she died because of a failure in her digestive system. I'd be lying if I said I wasn't still angry typing this over twenty years later, as the narcissistic part of me feels that God took her solely away from me. Don't worry; this is me just saying my truth aloud, and that transparency allows me to heal.

When my grandmother died, we attended a Catholic ceremony of course, but there wasn't a body because she had chosen to be cremated. I remember several people I did not know coming up and offering condolences to my father, brother, and me. As much as people come to comfort children at funerals, they never actually have a discussion with them about the traumatic event leading to the death of their loved one. It's mostly just grown-ups whispering, withholding information. I remember feeling like I had lost a limb since my grandmother was the direct link to my paternal family members, from my understanding of social issues, my interest in education, my connection to so much culture ... everything.

Yet this feeling was nothing new to me because I had just lost my favorite uncle, who was a designated replacement for my biological father, a couple of years prior. I believe I suppressed my traumatic experiences for so long that I can't recall exact dates or ages these events occurred. My uncle was the male equivalent of the way I viewed my grandmother. As my biological father's brother, he was his polar opposite: charming, outgoing, driven, adventurous, and accomplished. I'm pretty sure he was gay, but he never confirmed it. He wasn't feminine, but we always hung out with him and his White roommate named Mike. Mike was a huge, hairy White guy, who I know now would be affectionately titled a bear. My brother and I counted down the days until we got to spend the weekend at their house, because we knew it would be an adventure. My uncle basically treated us like his children because he didn't have any. He took us places we would have never gone otherwise, such as Space Center Houston, museums, and renaissance festivals. He tried teaching us how to drive in his really cool candy-red Jeep when I was only about twelve years old. He talked to me about education and even had me looking at colleges and universities. He was the person who made me truly believe that I could be anything and do anything I wanted to, with the right amount of effort. He was into physical health and wellness. He worked out regularly and ate well. He was a perfect human being in my eyes. I felt that as long as I had my grandmother and uncle in my life, the future looked bright.

Within a year, I saw my uncle go from a muscular and fit man to an unrecognizable version of himself. He would still come pick us up on weekends, but the visits were shorter and less adventurous. He stayed in his room more and more, leaving Mike to entertain us. I started to sense something was wrong when he began to lose several pounds and seemed to have lost the joy in his once illuminated eyes.

Once again, no one talked to us about what he was experiencing, not even him. The weekend visits eventually stopped altogether, and I remember feeling hurt and confused. He would call to check on us via telephone but did not have much energy to carry a full conversation. I remembered hoping that whatever he was going through would be over by the holidays.

One day, my mother received a call from the family telling us to rush to the hospital to see my uncle. To my surprise, the visit would serve as an opportunity to say my last goodbyes. Turns out my uncle had been in the hospital, dying slowly, which no one saw fit to tell my brother and me. They walked us into his hospital room and sat us next to his bedside. It pained me to see him with tubes running from every direction of his body. He could barely talk and seemed to be gasping for air. As an adult, I now know that he was taking his final breaths and saved them to say goodbye to us. When the shock wore off, I burst into tears and could not contain myself. My uncle mustered up enough energy to tell me he loved me and that he didn't want me to cry. "Don't cry," he said. "It's OK." It wasn't though.

I remember the adults in the room decided it was time for my brother and me to leave, but I wasn't ready to go. They ushered us out of the room, and I went reluctantly, looking back with terror in my eyes. As I am writing this, I realized that I haven't even typed his name because doing so brings the pain rushing back. Mark. His name was Uncle Mark.

My grandmother took us to the chapel and helped us say a prayer. As usual, she was strong and did not waver in her faith. We sat in that chapel for some time until they came back to tell us that he was gone. All the trauma I have endured in my lifetime combined pales in comparison to this tragedy. In another book at another time, I will explain how this led to years of anger, anxiety, and attachment issues, but for now, I will just say it really messed me up.

You may be wondering why I am sharing stories of death and dying with you in regard to spirituality, but one of the most important ideas we struggle with in the spiritual arena is mortality. No matter how physically fit we are or how well we eat, we all have an expiration date. No matter how much we love someone or feel we need them in our lives, they will eventually leave us, or we will leave them.

So, although I do not identify with a specific practice of religion, I find strength and peace in the concept of spirituality. Once you understand and acknowledge that the body is temporary but the soul lives forever, you begin to realize that all of it matters and none of it matters. As a therapist, it's hard to watch people get so caught up in physical and material things that they completely miss out on the opportunity to connect with the energy around them. I am a person who views energy as a sort of spiritual connectedness.

I wasn't sure how I was going to get the little spirituality I had back after the deaths of several important people in my life. It was reminiscent of a Solange song: I tried to sleep it away, pray it away, dance it away. It certainly wasn't from lack of trying. I tried to attend churches of different denominations or no denomination at all. It would always start off cool, but then it would get awkward, or something would turn me off. I remember going to one church I really enjoyed—until they started live Tweeting and asking us to take photos with our neighbors to post and tag the church in. I realized that I enjoyed being a student, so I didn't need all the glitz and glamor when I attended church because I was simply seeking understanding.

After that, I took a break from church and tried other ways to connect spiritually, including yoga and meditation. I will say that yoga helps me feel at peace and connect with my inner self, which is an important part of the spiritual journey that people miss. After doing a series of poses, we would sit with our legs crossed in a meditative state and remain silent for some time. It's amazing how relaxed and clear your mind becomes as a result. Yoga was and is certainly helpful but maybe just wasn't enough. I also tried still meditation, which was very difficult for me as a person with adult ADHD. However, when I joined Tai Chi, I was able to learn about moving meditation, which is very effective. My very first yoga instructor took a special liking to me, probably because I was young and a woman of color. Most of my classmates were upper-middle class, older White people. He invited me to a special weekend class pretty much aimed at finding yourself. It was an eight-hour class where we had to do all types of activities but also learned about mind, body, and soul health. I felt really woke after that class and continued to be mentored by him. He made me come in at six in the morning before work to teach me the wonders of moving meditation. It really helped, but there was no way I was making it there every morning at six. In our regular classes, we learned about how to control energy, and we made giant energy balls. If you haven't done this, you should try; it can be enlightening. It was during my time in Tai Chi that I realized that everything you're searching for outside of yourself can probably be found inside. I learned to find pleasure in the simplest things and understood the power of a minimalist lifestyle.

HIP-HOP SAVED MY LIFE

With all of my adventures in the search for true spirituality, it finally hit me that the source of spirituality was there with me the whole time. Going back to church, I remember the most powerful moments for me were in the choir, singing passionately and in unison. This was the only time I felt the tingling of the holy spirit. Even though I was never really taught about the contents of the Bible, one thing that was easy to resonate with was the joyful spirit of the music throughout the sermon. It's amazing that a song can capture everything you didn't even know you were feeling and thinking all at once. Even when you don't even know the words! Now that's power.

I started writing poetry around age eleven or twelve to express my pain and frustration with the world around me. It was cool, but it wasn't until I figured out how to match those rhymes to hip-hop beats that it became a healing tool for me. Although I really wanted to sing R&B like my favorite singer, Coko of *SWV*, God had a different plan for me. I wasn't raised around hip-hop culture per se, like my friends on the East Coast. I was more or less sheltered in my neighborhood because my mother didn't really let us go outside or be social. However, I had a very nice boombox, and I would sit and listen to the radio for hours. I eventually fell in love with the flows of artists like UGK, Tupac, Queen Latifah, Biggie, and Snoop Dogg. I began to study their style and cadence, eventually developing my own stage personality. My first performance arena was my bedroom, and it eventually moved to the fireplace area in the living room. I would order CDs, especially with instrumental versions so that I could add my own verses and maybe even a hook.

Since the beginning of my career in music, I have wanted to utilize the gift to educate and spread positive messages to the people. I suppose that influence comes directly from my grandmother, the community activist. I never even thought about making money from it or being famous; it was more of a spiritual experience. My mother took notice of my talent, however, and made me believe otherwise. I must give my mother credit for teaching me the can-do attitude and how to take control of my destiny. She quickly became my momanger, but that didn't last long. The fire fizzled out, and I began to focus on my studies.

While working on my dissertation in doctoral school, I remember being in a miserable state. I had absolutely no interest in writing a dissertation but was eager to get to the community and apply my therapeutic skills. After all, my grandmother needed exactly zero degrees to accomplish the great things she did. I seriously thought about quitting, which was ridiculous to most because I had already finished all the doctoral course work and was on the second chapter of my dissertation. Who does that?

One day, I was trying hard to focus on my dissertation but was not in a good place after just getting out of a long relationship. I was already at my wit's end with correcting the current chapter and had all but checked out of the doctoral process. I started to wonder why I was even doing it since my master's degree and license were sufficient for what I wanted to do in the field of mental health. I realized I was doing it for my family, as the first one to graduate from a university and get any type of degree. That was fine and dandy, but I had to reckon with the fact that I had absolutely no desire to complete the dissertation and was not happy. In a moment of clarity, I closed my computer and grabbed a notepad. I heard the song "Crush on You" with the epic Lil' Kim verse and took it as a sign. I started writing a breakup song to the very same beat and instantly felt rejuvenated. I probably hadn't written a song since I was a teenager. The lyrics I wrote were not life altering, but it was rather the spiritual experience I had from physically writing the words. I don't need to tell you that I never looked at that dissertation again. It was music and mental health from then on, and I felt more alive than I ever had before.

So, to be clear, I'm not knocking the church, religion, or anything in between. However, I do want to encourage any person identifying with this experience to keep searching until you find what's right for you. There is not one way to have a spiritual journey, no matter what anyone says. It can be found in nearly any and everything around you if you open your heart to the experience. You and only you will know when you have found it because your soul will feel complete. You will begin to vibrate on a higher wavelength and gain clarity on your purpose.

As my following grows, I am finding that music is certainly its own form of ministry. Having performed in front of fifty, five hundred, five thousand, and even fifty-thousand-plus people, it is very clear that I am not alone in feeling a special connection to music and lyrics. Several times after my show, I have been approached by someone in tears, saying the lyrics and music really resonated with them. Some people have written to me on social media, saying that my album helps them get through the dark times and find light. Others say that music inspires and empowers them to follow their passion and let go of fears. The exchange of energy during a live concert is one of the most exhilarating experiences one will ever have. So, if I never get a hit record or win an award, I will still feel accomplished and complete.

The closure I could not get from my losses was resolved through song. The anger, hurt, and pain from my past was able to be addressed. Most importantly, it allowed me to share the lessons I learned and create positive messages of healing through hip-hop for others to heal too.

"Relax" by Genesis Blu

I am not a profit, a preacher, a psychic a teacher
I'm just trynna wake you up before Joe Black comes
to meet ya
The finally's coming soon, you better make your
feature
Keep movin' you can't freeze
Life control alt deletes ya', depletes ya
So get on your grind
Make haste, expedience, cause you livin' on
borrowed time
I'm trynna prosper through suppression, while
surviving through the pain
This ain't a different world Dwayne, we livin the
same thing
And I'm just trynna keep my head above water and
maintain
Speak truth to Lost Ones before they label me
insane
This is that cruising through your city music,
whippin wood grain
And I'm just glad to be here so I ain't gon' complain
Hook
Relax, Relate, Release the stress
Know the trials and tribulations before you are just
a test
The body's temporary but the soul is endless
So relax, relate, release and be blessed

You can sink or swim in this ocean of life, why don't
you dive in?
Recognize the difference between livin and survivin
Thrivin, instead of bending over and complying
Apathy throughout this generation keeps me sighing
but I am
Trynna be a breath of fresh air
And though the stress get overwhelming stay cool
and debonair
But at the same time make sure you're reaching
your potential
The pursuit of happiness in this life is so essential
Now take care of your body, don't forget about the
mental
Cuz it's more about the journey and less about your
credentials
The future is before you so don't look behind
And take the shackles off your feet so you can free
your mind

IT'S BLUMING SEASON

Whether you are just beginning your journey of self-discovery or
are stuck somewhere in the middle, the good news is it's always a
good time for growth. I like to call this period *Bluming season*. No
matter where we are in life, we can choose to begin a new journey,
from going back to school or starting a new business to trying a new
hobby. We have been taught that you may be too old, too late, or
too messed up to follow your passion. This is simply not the case,
as I can recount hundreds if not thousands of stories with people
Bluming in the middle or later on in life. Typically, the greatest
obstacle with many people is overcoming fear of the unknown,

which is interesting to me because most religious or spiritual people claim to have complete faith. I call BS because faith and fear cannot occupy the same space.

In addition, it should be noted that the most beautiful and precious things in life often include a labor of love. Thinking about nature, a butterfly goes through a gruesome process in order to transform into its extravagant state. I often ponder about the amount of blood, sweat, and tears that must have been shed to build the pyramids in Egypt. Getting to your Bluming season will and should be a labor of love, as I am sure you have heard that anything worth having is worth working for. Is your happiness worth it?

I decided a long time ago that my happiness was absolutely worth anything and everything, so I took a chapter from the Book of Badu and started to unload my baggage. You must pack lightly if you want to have a successful journey; otherwise you will just be weighed down by the struggles of your past. The beauty is that you totally get to decide what baggage to take and which to leave behind. For anyone who has had difficulty letting go of the past hurt or refusing to practice forgiveness, know that your spirit dies a little each time you continue to replay that trauma in your mind. One of my mentors used to say this quote, I don't know from where, that put it so succinctly it stuck with me to this very day: "Holding on to hurt and anger is like you drinking poison every day and waiting on the other person to die." Read that again.

Listen, I could be angry with my mother, father, cousins, uncle, grandmother, and even with God. I could really live in it because I have every right to do so. However, I choose to relinquish the anger and hurt because it has not served a positive purpose in my life. Instead, I choose to understand that my family members did the best they could with whatever hand was dealt to them. My grief, although painful, was not personal. We all have to leave, and as much as God has allegedly taken, He has given ten times over.

I choose to let go of the bad to make room for more good. I choose to honor the legacy of lost ones and create relationships that fulfill emotional and spiritual needs. No, the pain did not disappear; I'm just no longer drinking the poison, and that was my choice.

BLU'S RULES FOR SLAYING LIFE

1. Never compare yourself to others.
2. If you fail, fail *forward*.
3. Personalize your definitions of love, success, and happiness.
4. You are not an island; build a healthy support system.
5. You are responsible for your happiness.
6. Surround yourself with people who are going where you want to go or have already arrived.
7. Thoughts become things, so be mindful.
8. Passion breeds purpose. Find yours.
9. The best of business, in the line of business, is to mind *your* business.
10. Only light can conquer darkness, so be light.
11. Tend to the mind, body, and soul as much as possible.
12. Go. To. Therapy.

Add Your Own:
13.

PART 3

Be Courageous Anyway

There is no better time than the present to pour myself on to the pages of this book with reckless abandon, because my mission in life is to give back to others. As I open up my heart to be transparent with you, I pray that you open your heart to be transparent with yourself. There is no cookie-cutter method to becoming the best you that you can be. No matter where you are on your journey, one of the keys to experiencing greater is being open to the idea that greatness is inside of you. It may be dormant. It may be silenced. It may be suffocating and drowning because of all the things that you have been through, but I want you to know that it is in there. You are one step away from walking in your greatness, and that one step is changing your perspective of who you are and who you are truly meant to be. What I am asking you to do right now, no matter where you find yourself at this moment, is to *be courageous anyway*!

Courage is not the absence of fear. Courage is deciding to move forward no matter what is terrorizing you. The thing most of us fear is a manifestation of something that is greater than what we think we have the ability to do, based on our current circumstances. If you are anything like me, you may feel like the odds are stacked against you and that it is too late. It's not too late, because you are here now reading this. Every person I know has their own unique set of circumstances that are sprinkled with the commonality of our humanity. Our humanity, however, has limitations. Look beyond those limitations and see through to the essence of who you truly are—a spiritual being having a human experience.

When we look at where we come from, where we are today, and where we want to be, it can be overwhelming. How can we tackle such a daunting task that requires so much of us? I say we will tackle that task one step at a time. Let's focus less on the destination and enjoy the journey. You can have an endgame in mind, but if your perspective is jaded, you won't discern that each step you're taking has the power to lead you to where you are meant to be. Imagine if we allowed ourselves the power of embracing the moment and believing that we will get there if we remain diligent. Endurance is more important than time and speed. The race will be won by those who endure. For this journey, I want you to view yourself as a triathlete competing in a triathlon. A triathlon is an athletic event that consists of three different parts, usually swimming, cycling, and long-distance running. In this case, I want you to think of the three parts in this reference: spirit, mind, and body. Also, keep in mind that you are your only competition. Your only mission is to complete becoming your best self.

My faith teaches me that I am a spirit, I possess a mind, and my mind and spirit are housed inside of my body. At times, we can be stronger in one area than we are in another. The beauty is we have the ability to effectively change the condition of those three areas when we make a decision to do so. If you are depleted in your spirit, you can do things to nourish it. If you are fatigued in your mind, you can do things to strengthen it. Your body is also subject to change when you apply the right principles to transform it. Outside forces may influence us to seek those changes, but ultimately the desire to change must come from within. I am reminded of a scripture that says, "As a man thinking in his heart so is he" (Proverbs 23:7). The thoughts we have about ourselves speak louder than any words spoken to us from outside voices. To be courageous anyway, we must deal with the voices that say, "You are less than, versus greater than."

Voices have spoken to me throughout my life, and I have allowed voices both negative and positive to decide which step I would take. Needless to say, when I have followed the voices of negativity, they have led me down the wrong path. The interesting thing about going down the wrong path is that it never changes the destination we were originally designed to reach. Any wrong turn in our lives can be used as a lesson if we allow it to be. At the age of forty-four, I am reminded that my purpose, no matter where I have gone and what I have been through, has not changed. In actuality, adversities and my own hardheadedness have instead made me more determined to reach for my goals with all that I have in me. I believe you are determined to reach for your goals too. Let US reach for our goals together. US stands for *unity* and *strength*. Women have that power. We have the power to unite and strengthen one another. That is what we are doing here. What we think is powerful. It is time we change our thinking.

A little over a decade ago, I rediscovered my purpose. There were glimpses of it all throughout my childhood, but I have come to understand that a molestation in my formative years attempted to assassinate my dreams early on. My childish mind was molded by this disgusting act perpetrated against me. What I didn't know then is that it was a tool used to shape what I thought of myself and what I believed about my potential.

An eight-year-old little girl has no control over her environment and the people who are in it. As I look back, I can identify when my self-worth became damaged, but this is my forty-four-year-old self, looking back on my adolescence. For many years, I wondered what was wrong with me, and I felt like I was a bad person, not worthy of the best. Those negative thoughts shaped the steps I took for the vast majority of my life. There were times I felt good about things I accomplished, but there was a voice lying underneath the surface (for more than three decades) that shouted, "You really aren't good."

Have you ever felt like you are pretending and that one day the charade would be up and you would be exposed for being the miserable, no-good person you really are? If you said yes or you can relate to that in the least, chances are you have a voice from your past that thinks it is welcome in your future. Today is your day to answer that voice! Tell that voice to go to hell! That's exactly where it belongs. There is no sugarcoating it. You can't passively dismiss it any longer. You can't let it keep whispering sweet nothings in your ear. You have to speak to it and tell it to shut the hell up! Choose courage in the face of this nasty assault against who you truly are. That is not just negative self-talk; it is an evil spiritual force designed to keep your head cloudy and your decision-making shaky. When you stand up against it and demand that it not only be silenced but go away, you unlock the door to a new path of confidence and surety.

Be sure that you are destined for greatness. You are. Be warned: your greatness is not to be compared with others. Comparison is a path that leads to desolation. The only measuring up you need to do is to your individual, God-given, custom-designed purpose. No one on this planet can do you like you. Period. When you embrace you, you embrace the spirit that is in you and all that it was purposed to accomplish during its journey through physical time. Our culture puts so much emphasis on time that time becomes a distraction to what is meaningful and purposeful. There is no perfect age to get married, start a career, have children, climb a mountain, or set the world ablaze. Be it unto you according to your faith. If you believe you can conquer the world at eighteen ... you can. If you wake up at fifty and decide it's time to set the record straight ... it is. The time constraints that we force ourselves to follow are ego driven not purpose driven. Again, the most important thing is endurance. If you are a teenager, you will have to endure. If you are a seasoned woman, you will have to endure. Endurance/stamina is something you must train for.

Again, I want you to think about an athlete preparing for a triathlon. Do you think that athlete can just wake up one morning, go out, and finish each event successfully without training? I won't insult your intelligence because I know that you know better. The athlete who chooses to enter the race, no matter how old he/she/they are, must prepare themselves to finish. They must go out and practice swimming. They must learn different techniques. They must go through various exercises and experiences in the water. Eventually, through rigorous training, practices, and failures, they will be prepared to take on the real challenge and win. If they stop there and don't prepare for the cycling and running portion of the event, they will fall short. Working in one area and neglecting the others will only lead to disappointment. Let me reiterate, as I may do from time to time, that we are taking things one step at a time. The athlete can't swim, run, and ride a bicycle all at once. They must pay special attention to each individual area. Paying special attention to each area will have a domino effect, however. The stamina built while cycling will impact the stamina needed for running and so forth.

As women, we have had the idea of being able to multitask shoved down our throats. We are often shamed if we are not doing a million things at one time. We are shamed if we say no to something we don't want to do. Because, by God, "we are every woman," and we should be able to do everything. I say wrong. There is nothing wrong with being multitalented. I believe an overwhelming majority of us have to be just to survive. However, I submit that it is OK if we choose to focus on one thing at a time. The skills I sharpen in one area can spill over into other areas of my life, but it is perfectly fine to let people know … right now I'm focused on this. Whatever that *this* is for you, work that thing.

In 1994, I was fresh out of high school and decided to attend Sam Houston State University. At that time in my life, I was bogged down with the weight that was baggage from my past. I didn't know it then, but my careless behavior put my baggage front row and center in my life. I was eighteen, still carrying around the stench of a molestation that had very much shaped my subconscious thinking. Promiscuity was wrecking my life, and it wasn't asking for permission. As a matter of fact, I had given it full leeway to do as it pleased. One night, I was at my wit's end with myself, and I began to ask God what was wrong with me. For the first time in my life, I wanted to understand what I was doing and how I had arrived at such a self-destructive place.

Those questions started the process of peeling away the layers of years of hurt and confusion. The abuse I had suffered came back to me vividly. I became angry, and I wanted more answers. On a trip home, one weekend, I decided I wanted to sit down with my parents and discuss what I knew had happened to me. We did. It was painful. They listened. They provided feedback, and that one conversation didn't solve all of my problems, but I know now it set me on a different path. A path that said to me suppression of trauma is not the answer. Pretending things never happened won't solve anything because you still have to live with the scars. My scars manifested in a multitude of ways, and the majority of those manifestations were not positive, but there is one scar that brings out my beauty. The soft tissue of the greatness in me lies right below the surface of that scar. This scar produced a desire in me to help others. I don't want to see other young people … especially young women … go through what I have gone through.

Cultivating that desire is part of my training. We must cultivate the right desires in our lives. Let me bring clarity to what I mean. To do that, I will continue to expound on my adolescent years. Writing has been my cathartic release from the pain. Poetry was one of the first outlets that allowed me to release what I was feeling inside. Connecting to this gift has been a pathway to my freedom. Sharing this gift with others is a key to my divine destiny. Here is a cleansing poem that I wrote many years ago when I was a young girl.

"Put It Behind"

Reminiscing for the soul can be deadly
The horrible past can make the heart cold
Those that can't move on grow a heart of stone
Seize the day
Don't let time run its race
Face tomorrow with a running pace
Hope for a loving future and turn against a lonely past
Don't compare or contrast your future to your past
Build your life on a future that will last
Remember your destiny … you control
Don't live your life regretting
Move on

This poem is relevant because it points me back to my purpose. See, all along, my spirit was taking notes. It was leaving messages for me to find my way back to who I really am. What message is your spirit trying to communicate with you? You have to train yourself to listen to your spirit. Have you ever heard the saying *children are resilient*? This is often referenced when children have gone through traumatic experiences. It is expected that children have the innate ability to bounce back from the harshest of circumstances. I won't disagree with that. I will endeavor to say what is actually resilient is the spirit of a child.

Again, we are a spirit. We possess a soul, and that spirit and soul is housed inside of a body. Your spirit has a built in ability to fight. That built-in ability is called faith. It is imperative that you not allow your spirit/faith to be broken. (But even if your spirit is broken, there is hope. Your spirit may be broken; it *cannot* be destroyed. It *can* be healed.) This is why we are encouraged to fight the good fight of faith (1 Timothy 6:12). That is truly the only fight we can win. When your spirit soars, you soar. My spirit knew exactly who I was even when my mind didn't. When my mind was cloudy because of the things that had happened to me, my spirit was keeping an accurate record of who God created me to be.

Cultivating the desire to discover who I am opened me up to hear my spirit. My spirit was able to lead me back to my purest, most innocent self. Train yourself to listen to your spirit. The courage that you need to move forward is housed inside of that resilient spirit. Adversities in your life are designed to kill your spirit, but that tiny seed of faith that was placed there by your Creator will spring forth as you begin to train it.

You can train your spirit by feeding it the right thing. The more you feed it, the stronger it will become. Feast on positivity. Feast on what the Creator has said about you. The more you feast on what the Creator says ... the smaller the negative voices of your past will become. The Creator tells us to think on what is lovely and what is pure (Philippians 4:8). He wants you to think on what is praiseworthy. Can you write down ten things about yourself that are praiseworthy? Give it a shot. This is a part of your triathlon training.

1.

2.

3.

4.

5.

6.

7.

8.

9.

10.

Train yourself to see the good in you. The more of the good you can see in you, the more it will manifest on the outside. Don't be distracted by old thoughts. Push pass them. They are only trying to hinder your discovery. On this journey, you are tasked with the job of discovering what your gift/gifts are. Tapping into your gift/gifts opens new doors to you that only you possess the keys to. The truth is you possess everything you need to succeed. It's time to awaken it. Warm it up like you would do your muscles before a workout.

Imagine getting up in the morning with those ten praiseworthy things on your mind to start the day. How would that change your perspective and how you approach each day? I'll share my list of ten praiseworthy things with you.

1. I am Patrina.
2. I am an awesome writer.
3. I am the greatest creative writer in the world.
4. I am making dynamic strides in my writing.
5. I am able to create interesting, dynamic, and captivating moments in my writing.
6. I love my craft.
7. I perfect my craft.

8. I love God.
9. I am grateful for every moment.
10. I communicate authentically, and I have a remarkable understanding.

Your list is not to be compared to mine. Your list is your list. It provides you with the nourishment you need to continue to train and stay motivated to endure.

After traveling down many dark paths, I finally started to walk down a path that was illuminated for me. Psalms 119:105 says, "Your word *is* a lamp to my feet And a light to my path." It took me growing through some things to get there. At the age of twenty-one, I became pregnant for the first time. I wasn't married, but I knew that the person growing inside of me deserved me living at a higher level than what I was doing at the time. One thing is for sure ... some drastic changes were in order. My spirit was stirring up and demanding that I change. Demanding that I do better. Be better for me and be better for my unborn child.

The Creator used my pregnancy to transform my lifestyle (light my path). I let go of everything and everyone who wouldn't encourage me to stay on the right path. On the outside looking in, it appeared I was making another huge mistake. I got married (I am now twice divorced). I don't look at the marriage(s) as a mistake. It gave me the opportunity I needed to get rooted and grounded. I was devoted to raising my son and being the best mother I could be. My life slowed down a lot. It needed to. The desire for change led me to the scriptures of the Holy Bible and self-help books. My faith begin to develop by what I was reading and through what I was hearing.

Church(es) have gotten a bad rap over the past ... let's say two decades or more—some for good reason. I won't say every experience that I have had in church has been great, but what I will say is that there were things that were offered at my church that changed my life in a positive way, and I know for sure I wouldn't have done it without it. For example, the women's ministry in the church I attend was phenomenal. Spiritually, they taught me how to connect with God, and they encouraged me to seek God about my life's purpose. They gave me biblical principles and practical ways to apply those principles.

I was a young, stay-at-home wife and mother. My family was rapidly growing. I have three biological children who kept me very busy, and I poured all the love I could into them. As an individual, I wanted something for myself. I needed something for me. I attended the women's meetings, hungry for what I would discover each time, and eventually I became involved in a leadership role. This was my outlet outside of my home—a way a could connect with other women who were likeminded, and I could receive mentorship. All were very important for my spiritual growth. (Don't get sidetracked. We are still talking about the triathlon and training. More is caught than taught. So close pay attention.)

We would have monthly fellowships and planning meetings. There were times when we were able to travel and attend other women's meetings/conferences. I was being ignited to seek my purpose wholeheartedly, and I was being exposed to tools that would help me excavate the treasures that were in me. I began to explore what I liked and didn't like. What moved me and what didn't. I started moving back to my first love … creative writing. Through volunteer opportunities, I began writing short plays that complemented the women's meetings/conferences. I linked up with someone in the ministry who was just as passionate about writing as I was. What started out as short skits expanded into ten-minute plays. Ten-minute plays evolved into full-length plays. It wasn't long before I started writing and producing plays for other events in the church as well. The creative arts ministry started coming alive, and it was drawing the young people to participate. The more I did it, the more I realized how much I loved it. My writing was giving me a platform to work with the people I wanted to help.

On the surface, it may look like I am saying my purpose is to be a creative writer, but that is not what I am saying. I am a creative writer, but my purpose is to bring light where there is darkness. Because I am a creative writer, I use that ability to fulfill my purpose. The things that happened to me as a child were trying to steal that purpose and silence my voice. That is the purpose of anything evil. It is there to steal away that which is purposed and to silence it from speaking up in a helpful way. The courage I had/have to actualize my true self transcends those evil intentions. This is why again I say, "Be courageous anyway."

Getting around the right people in a season when I needed it the most pulled out the greatness that is in me. Pulling it out wasn't enough though. That was just the surface work, but the surface is where you dive in. Through the spirit, you are able to dig deeper, but you have to ask the question: what lies beneath? There are layers to you. You are more than just your skin, your hair, your waist, your weight on the scale, the size of your feet, the color of your eyes, the sound of your voice. Did I miss anything? How do you summarize who you are? Are you just the kids' mom? Are you just your husband's wife? Are you just your mother's daughter? Who are you underneath all of those labels? Me ... I'm an artist. A creative artist. A creative artist who loves to write. But more importantly, I am a creative artist who loves to write and who loves inspiring people to shift from a place of darkness to a place of illumination.

Spirit ... you also were granted entry into this earth to do something purposeful. Underneath everything that you have been through and every title you have worn, you have a destiny. Who are you, and what is your purpose here on this earth? I want you to stop reading for five minutes and just meditate on that. Set a timer. Breathe and just meditate on that last question. After the timer goes off, take some time to write what you heard while you were meditating. It doesn't matter what you heard ... just write it. I want you to do this exercise every day until you have a clear, precise answer.

You are divine. Don't worry. If you didn't get the answer the first time, it will come because you are seeking. You are knocking. Matthew 7:7 (NLT) says, "Keep on asking, and you will receive what you ask for. Keep on seeking, and you will find. Keep on knocking, and the door will be opened to you." I can say that this is the honest-to-God Gospel Bill truth. God loves to answer our questions. Some of us are just afraid to ask. This is your season to choose courage. Ask, seek, and knock!

As I was telling you, the more I wrote plays, the more I loved it. I can go back to a memory in my childhood that reminds me of the joy I have when I write a play now. In the seventh grade, we did a creative writing exercise, and I'll never forget how happy I felt. That's all I wanted to do. As time continues to pass, I know more and more this is all I want to do with my life. I love it. You should love what you do. Your spirit should leap for joy about your life's work. No matter how many difficult days I have ... no matter the trials I face ... no one can take that joy from me. It is on the inside of me. Each project is a new opportunity to dig more into who I am and what I am capable of. My reach to inspire others keeps expanding. I am accomplishing my life's mission one step at a time.

Discovering that I can use my gift to write plays has been a game changer for me. I want to make sure I point out that this discovery happened while I was serving someone else. While I was attending meetings ... while I was going through training and helping someone else accomplish their mission and goals. While I was serving, room was being made for me because I wanted to find ways that I could contribute. If you are not finding ways to give of yourself to help others, you are stifling your discovery and growth.

Giving to others is rewarding, and it's a spiritual principle. Give, and it will be given to you. "They will pour into your lap a good measure—pressed down, shaken together, and running over [with no space left for more]. For with the standard of measurement you use [when you do good to others], it will be measured to you in return" (Luke 6:38 AMP).

My production company, The Fierce Arts and Entertainment Group, was birthed out of me using my gift to give back. I went from doing plays for the church for free to producing plays and selling tickets. The very first ticketed show I did in 2009, on Mother's Day weekend, sold out. I was able to pay the performers and crew. I invested my own money into it, and when the show was over, I had money left to invest in my next show. It was a hit! That was all the evidence I needed to know I was on the right track.

Producing that show wasn't without adversities, but the confidence I gained is something that was worth every challenge I went through. Shortly after producing that show, my marriage to my first husband went under fire, and we didn't make it through as a couple. That relationship was trying to rob me of my joy (the joy I discovered in operating in my purpose), but I refused to let go of what I had found. There was no way I could turn loose what God had given me. I determined that no one and nothing would take what I had sought after. Either you support me for who I am or you have to move out of the way and watch me fulfill my purpose from a distance. We divorced. I stumbled a bit. I was devastated, and once again I was hurt.

Through that devastation and hurt, I poured into myself into another area of my life that was spiraling out of control. I started to put myself first again. Over the course of that marriage, I had managed to put on more than a hundred pounds. Physically, I was in the worst shape of my life, and one day I became determined to fix that. I went on a new journey (it started before we were divorced). My new journey was to lose weight. That took a lot of mental stamina, spiritual searching, and physical sacrifice. I went all the way in.

I needed a positive accountability partner. I refused to be held back. I started searching for someone who could help me. Over the years, I had tried numerous things, but it wasn't until I became fed up that I found what worked. I refused to care what anyone thought … even the people closest to me. I found a personal trainer who was willing to work with me. I made adjustments in my finances to afford the training. One of the most radical things I did was cut my hair completely off. Cutting my hair off was liberating and saved me money. The money I saved was redirected to pay the trainer. Instead of spending that money in the salon, I spent it at the gym. I loved my fade and wore it proudly.

We trained three days a week. I slowly implemented nutritional changes. It helped to have a sister who was a nutritionist and gave me tips on how to adjust my eating habits. Back then, I was addicted to Little Debbie snacks. I would secretly eat boxes of Swiss rolls to comfort me emotionally, and it was definitely showing. My commitment to myself in this area paid off big-time. I went from wearing a size twenty-four to wearing a size ten. All of that was earned with dedication to making myself a priority.

I documented my journey through pictures and started sharing them on social media. Sharing my journey on social media inspired others and gave me a new outlet for my creativity. As I progressed on that journey, a friend of mine encouraged me to write a book about it. Years before, I had set a goal to write a book, but I never imagined that it would be about a weight-loss journey. In the midst of diving into health and fitness, I found out my father needed a kidney transplant. The Creator God always has a bigger plan in mind. There I was putting myself first for a change, and He still had someone else in mind.

Losing weight opened the possibility of me being a donor for my father. When I started out working on myself, there was no clue that the path would lead me there. Roughly, five thousand people (on the transplant list) die per year while waiting to receive a kidney transplant. If I had not started my transformation to lose weight, I would not have been an eligible candidate to donate a kidney to my father. Training and losing weight made me look better. It made me feel better, but it also gave me the opportunity to do something more profound. My commitment to the weight-loss process began in November 2008. Four years later, on November 13, 2012, I donated a kidney to my father. Not only was I a perfect match, but I was at a healthy weight to do it (obese people are rejected for donations because of the high risk for complications). The Creator made a way out of no way ... even when I didn't know He was making a way.

That story became a significant part of the book I was writing. Everything was coming full circle. I wrote the book *From Fat to Fierce* and released it in January 2013 as a part of my birthday celebration. The original title was *From Fat to Fine,* but once I released photos on social media from my photoshoot, people kept commenting the word *fierce.* A bell went off in my spirit, and I started connecting the dots. Fierce! That was my word. It described me. It embodied everything that I had been through up to that point, and I knew it would describe me walking through any new obstacles that come my way.

My brand was birthed! The very essence of who I am as a creative artist can be expressed in one word: *fierce*! Training spiritually prepared me to make the connection. Tune into the things that flow ... the things you don't have to force. Opportunities are going to present themselves. Be prepared. Plenty of the days spent in the gym included me praying to make it through my workouts. All of it was a setup for something greater.

Let's take a moment for me to recap and expound. When I was

an adolescent, I discovered a love for writing. Actually, I created performances and put on concerts for my parents with original songs I wrote. That was my gift to them for anniversaries and birthdays. They would be summoned to the living room to watch me put on a show. That was where I found my happiness.

At eight years old, I was being molested by a seventeen-year-old family member. This abuse happened over the period of two years. I started to change. I was angry. I acted out. At some point, I began to suppress what happened to me. I tried speaking up, but that didn't work. I started hating myself. I thought I was ugly. I thought I was a bad person. The only outlet I had was writing. I kept a diary, and it was my safe place to write how I was feeling.

My love for creative writing was nurtured by my seventh-grade teacher. Creative writing exposed my joy. The joy that cannot be taken away from me, although the evil perpetrated against me desperately tried to rob me of my joy.

At the age of fourteen, I became promiscuous. I was desperately seeking love and acceptance. I wanted to fit in. The more I acted out, the more I was punished. There was no therapy for the abuse and trauma I had gone through. My abuser stayed in my life. He was a part of my family. I developed weird coping mechanisms. I looked up to him and even tried to protect him. His abuse stopped being physical, and it became verbal. He would put me down and bad-mouth me to others. I dealt with this behavior well into my adulthood.

In Christian faith, we are taught to forgive. I am cool with forgiving. Forgiveness is important, but forgiveness is not a pass for people to not be held accountable for their actions. Especially horrendous actions against children. He should have been held accountable for what he did, and I should have received the therapy I needed and deserved. Therapy and counseling are not terms I grew up hearing. To my dismay, there are still stigmas that surround the idea of seeking that type of help, but I would urge anyone who has hidden traumas, no matter how old the trauma is, to seek counseling. Seek healing.

I was very angry and resentful. My suppression could not mask that. It only allowed the anger and resentment to manifest in self-destructive behaviors. It is imperative that we not skirt past trauma. The sad part is I know I'm not an exception. My story resonates with countless people, both male and female. People who are sexually abused, in their innocence as children, are left to sort out the pieces in their minds. Unfortunately, this is far too common. The anger and resentment I felt toward the people I felt should have protected me was a toxic time bomb. It imploded.

It wasn't until I was in my second semester in college, pursuing a degree in communications, that I begin to feel the weight of something being wrong with me. (I thought I wanted to pursue journalism. Ultimately, I was pursuing partying. I earned a degree in it.) The pain I was inflicting on myself being wild and out of control was taking its toll on me. I had a conversation with God, asking Him what was wrong and why was I behaving the way I was. He answered. He took me back to those years of sexual molestation. I was horrified, crushed, and angry all over again. I went home and talked to my parents. That was the beginning of me peeling back the layers. It is still a process, and I can link many of my choices back to that violation of my innocence and the coping mechanisms I created. That was another opportunity to seek counseling, but I didn't. Things went back to usual, and my behavior didn't change for the better overnight.

I dropped out of college, went home, and tried to pick up the pieces, but I picked up a new habit while I was away—smoking weed. It's not up for debate with me. Weed is addictive, and it ruled my life. I loved getting high and couldn't wait to get high again. I found a part-time job and went to cosmetology school. While I was in school, I found a friend who loved weed as much as I did. Somehow, I magically always found the people who loved to smoke weed. I worked. Got an apartment with a friend and wild out. I wild out until I hit rock bottom. Men, liquor, money, music, and weed. That was all I cared about. I lost my job. I tried to maintain a little side hustle, but that wasn't enough to pay the rent. Sadly, after a series of unfortunate events, I tucked my tail and went back to my parents' home. One motto I live by is "no matter where you go, you are there." So you can move around ... you can run, but until you deal with you, nothing will change.

At one time, I tried my hand at rapping. Female rappers were getting raunchy and becoming more sexualized during that time, but my main gig was working in a salon as an assistant. So I was living at home, still going out partying and getting into nonsense. The people I surrounded myself with were like-minded. Everyone was focused on getting high. Thankfully, by the grace of God, I can say I just stuck with weed and didn't progress to anything harder. But being a weed head was doing more than enough damage to my life. Every day after work, I rushed to find the weed man. My life was void of any signs of purpose.

Things caught up with me. I was feeling really funny and out of sorts. I started talking to God again about the disgust I had with myself. One day, I was getting high with a friend, and he told me that I needed to slow down. He said I was moving too fast. The irony is that he was right there with me ... in the fast lane. His words pierced my heart, and I couldn't shake them. A short time after that encounter (I was still making my moves and doing my thing but at a little slower pace), I found out I was pregnant with my firstborn son. I had met a new guy. He just so happened to be an entrepreneur. We were kicking it, and then the next thing you know, I found out after all my years of frolicking ... I was expecting. I told you earlier this is the moment that changed my life. There was no way I would raise a child running around out in the streets. I didn't know what that looked like. My mom was a homemaker. That's what I knew. God used that moment to illuminate my path and to steer me in a different direction. I can't tell you all the things that I went through … all the things that I did, but I do hope you are getting the picture. I had to make an about-face.

Your circumstances may not be that dire, but whatever your set of circumstances are, they are yours. Don't run from them. Stop suppressing them. Deal with whatever is holding you at your current location. Confront whatever is holding you back. You deserve the freedom to pursue your best you—right now. I'm still in pursuit of my best me.

Have you confronted your past, or do you pretend it doesn't exist? My past is the very reason I know I was born to inspire people to come out of dark places and move into the light. What was covered up in my life was threatening my life. The battle of the mind is a fight that can only be won by faith. Trust and believe. I fight that battle daily, and I have sought out therapy. I've been able to release so much by opening up and talking to a counselor. Years of frustration with myself and disappointment have been released. I can't stress enough how much it is a daily thing. I'm still arriving. When you think you have arrived, keep pushing. I share my story because it heals me and it helps others.

Believe that you are worth fighting for. When no one else is fighting for you, fight for yourself. I can't define your dream(s) for you, but I'm telling you that when you act on that courage I'm speaking of, it will propel you toward your next step. Get moving. Moving will make you hungry for more. Writing skits wasn't enough. I needed to explore more options. I needed to make a bigger splash. My full-length plays started evolving as a result of my motion. I went from writing plays and using other people's music in them to writing full-length musicals with my own original music.

Over the years, I dreamt of going back to school. I literally would have dreams of me going back to Sam Houston State University. If there was a way that I could do it and support my three small children, I would have. All was not lost. I just had to find the right avenue. That avenue was going to community college. My determination wouldn't take no for an answer. Sam was out of reach, but Lone Star Community College was right in my backyard. It was online. My children were a little older now. I set a goal for myself and got enrolled. I had to get a temporary loan from my mom to pay the installment while I waited on financial aid, but I vowed not to let anything stop. It was also important for me to set an example for my kids. I wanted to earn my degree and let them know that anything is possible when you set your mind to it.

My mindset was shifting. For years, I was reinventing the wheel producing my stage plays, but I knew that if I could just get back in school, there would be opportunities for me to learn how to work smarter, not harder. I was writing, costuming, set designing, painting, building, promoting, advertising, casting, producing, and directing my plays. Don't get me wrong. I learned a lot, but there was still something missing ... my formal education. My last two semesters at Lone Star were spent driving over an hour to Montgomery County to attend classes in stage craft for theatre arts. I learned more about scenic design in two semesters than I had taught myself in the six years I had been producing shows. This was heaven to me, and I ate up all the knowledge. This experience was training me for my next level.

Graduating with my associates of arts in 2018 wasn't enough. Before graduation, I started searching out schools that would give me the opportunity to learn more about theatre. Two of my major goals were to sharpen my writing skills and to be in a diverse environment. After much seeking and asking questions, I decided to apply to the University of Houston's School of Theatre and Dance. They were offering a bachelor's of fine arts in playwriting and dramaturgy. The requirement for applying was to submit a portfolio, which included a play you had written, a video of your work, and a professional theatre reference. I had been preparing for this moment. I was ready. I submitted my work, and my professor from Lone Star submitted a reference letter on my behalf.

One the way to my face-to-face interview, I prayed and worshipped. My spirit was telling me that I was headed to where I belonged, that this place would be home for me. My interview went well, and shortly after that, I received my letter of acceptance into the program. That was one of the happiest days of my life. When your steps are ordered, you will have peace. The storms in my life were raging up like a category five hurricane, but I remained focused on the next step in my journey.

"Be courageous anyway" was birthed during those storms. I was achieving victory in this area and watching God shift things into place for me. At the same time, while I was finishing my degree at Lone Star, my second marriage crumbled. I had been sure this marriage was going to last, but I was wrong. There are a million reasons why it wasn't working, but ultimately, selfishness and betrayal sunk that ship. (Here is a little sidebar nugget. Unequally yoked doesn't just pertain to salvation. Don't be unequally yoked to someone who hasn't done the work to know who they are and who isn't actively pursuing their own fruitful purpose. You won't be able to walk together. Amos 3:3 says, "Can two walk together, except they be agreed?" I say it is impossible to walk with someone you can't agree with. You have to be on the same page.)

We went through a horrible and dramatic breakup. I was being gaslit, and, well, quite honestly, that only encouraged me to act a complete fool. This time, I was able to easily put my finger on the source of my choices. A harsh reality was there was still so much in me that didn't believe I deserve the best. I took my behind back to counseling. When we don't past certain tests in life, there will be a repeat. It was time for more soul searching. I couldn't solely put the blame on him. There were some tough questions I had to ask myself. Why did I feel the need to compromise my core values? was one of those questions. We all have a set of core values. When we violate those core values to have certain things in our lives, they are bound to backfire on us.

You cannot fool your spirit. Your spirit knows everything about you. Your spirit won't let you rest when you do things that oppose it. Temporary satisfaction for something that needs a permanent solution won't lead to perfect peace. It is an innate desire to dwell in peace. You can't invite turmoil into your life and expect it to bring anything other than havoc. The last thing you need on your journey is someone who counteracts everything you believe in. My evaluation of myself in those moments revealed that I was still living from a place of feeling I was not good enough. Those thoughts were still deeply rooted in my past experience. After speaking to my counselor, it was clear that I still needed to resolve the issues that were plaguing me. He advised me to write a letter to my abuser.

I followed his advice. When I finished writing the letter, it was seven pages deep. I discovered that I was wearing the guilt and the shame of what happened to me like a coat. It was time to take the coat off. The words in my letter released me from the need to cover and protect the person who violated me. Decades having passed by didn't remove the pain or its effects. Time does not heal all wounds. Time can bury them, but they are still there, waiting to be triggered. I decided not to spare his feelings. Wrapping things up in fluffy words to make him feel good would not resolve anything. This would be my proverbial day in court, when I could speak to my abuser and tell him exactly how I felt. Who knows? If I had done it years ago, it may have spared me all the anguish I put myself through. I will never know. What I do know is that I am grateful to have finally come to this point on my path.

After writing the letter, I put it in an envelope and carried it with me, determined to hand deliver it. Finally, one Sunday, I got my opportunity. I walked right up to him, gave him the letter, and walked away. Was I expecting an apology? No. I'll never know if he read it. Honestly, that is not the point. The letter was for me. Articulating what happened to me and the damage that it had done was me acknowledging that I know the source of my hurt. It also gives me my power back because, moving forward, I know that I need to make choices for myself that are healthy. I may not have been able to choose my path at eight years old, but I have the power and the wisdom to choose it now. I'm taking responsibility for who and what I allow in my life. If someone or something does not line up with what I have decided are my foundational values in life, I have the freedom to not engage. Exercise your personal freedom to accept and decline. Being molested tried to rob me of my power to say, "No!" Sexual acts being forced on me programmed me to think I had to accept anything a man offered me. That is a lie.

This is why I urged you in the beginning of my writing to be transparent with yourself. If there are still things holding you back or tripping you up, it is highly likely that they are connected to traumas from your childhood. Things may appear hopeless, and you may think that you will never overcome your demons, but you can. We can. Remember it is US. With unity and strength, we can conquer and defeat our self-sabotaging demons. Step by step.

There were times when I doubted myself for walking away from my second marriage. I spent some time thinking about what other people would think of me. There are people in our society who look down on divorcees. I've been privy to the judging and shaming comments about people who have married more than once. On several occasions, I had to deal with thoughts of rejection and unworthiness. You know those moments where we wallow in self-pity. Each time, I have had to shake myself and remember that I have always been worthy of being loved and protected. Regardless of what others think, I came to the realization that I am the one who has to live in my house. My house has to be a place where love and peace reside. Choose peace.

Maintaining my relationship with the Creator and encouraging myself in the Word was my lifeline through that valley. He has comforted me and guided me through the thick of it, even in the moments when I traveled backward to a familiar place. Letting go and moving forward doesn't come with a magic formula. It takes work to release the things in your life that are toxic. Sometimes we are intoxicated by the toxicity. It can creep in and become the norm. I am reminded of a quote from a powerful woman who I admire, Dr. Marina McLean, "Chaos doesn't know that it is chaos until order steps in."

Don't allow yourself to get comfortable with the chaos. Pay attention to the warning signs, and don't make excuses for your failure to heed them. When I asked Him for a sign, He laid it right in my lap. He will do that. He will illuminate a situation and make it so clear that if you don't see it, it's only because you refuse to. There is no amount of lies that can cover up the truth of what He is showing you. He ultimately wants the best for you, even when you don't want the best for yourself.

The things that we settle for don't stretch us. If we want to grow, we have accept the fact that there will be some growing pains. Saying no to things that aren't in our best interest will delay our gratification, but temporary gratification comes with insurmountable hardships. Avoiding the long route will have you going in circles. The children of Israel in the Bible are a prime example of this type of mindset. God delivered them from the hands of Pharaoh and led them out on a path to what He had promised them. However, every time they faced a challenge, they murmured, complained, and looked for an alternative route to God's plan. Their discontentment with following what God was orchestrating kept them wandering around in the wilderness for forty years. After all He had done for them, they still didn't trust Him. Make it a point to count your blessings. That is a part of your training too. We must train ourselves to be grateful. Gratefulness is the path to something greater.

Stepping on to the campus of UH was peaceful. My mental training for the next level of the game was essential. Wanting more requires more, and there were plenty of uncomfortable sacrifices I had to make to get it. There have been plenty of days when I've stepped on campus in the wee hours of the morning and didn't leave until the wee hours of night. I started doing this with a son budding into adulthood, a daughter who was a freshman in college (four and half hours away), and a younger son who was an athlete and a junior in high school. My children have seen me train for what I want. They were there when I earned my associate's degree. They have seen me build a show from the ground up, and by the grace of God, they will be here to see the fruit of my labor.

Classes started for me at UH in August 2018. The university offered me courses in every area of theatre, including acting (being a playwright doesn't start and stop with writing a play). There are many facets of theatre for me to learn about. They in turn will help me be a better writer. Natural talent is good, but I believe when you are great, it is because you have put in the necessary time to study your craft and hone your skills. I'm still putting in my ten thousand hours to earn my expertise in my field. That's time invested in my personal growth. Grow forward.

This is not the season to wallow in what might have been. It is the season to pursue purpose with fierce determination. Grab your dreams by the handful and write them down. Make the vision plain (Habakkuk 2:2). That is part of the process that takes what is in your heart and mind and makes it visual. I surround myself with images and confessions that will produce what I want to see. This intake is propelling me toward the right people, the right places, and the right things. That doesn't happen by accident, and best believe it won't happen without opposition. There is not a week that goes by that something doesn't pop up to challenge my commitment to my purpose. We are battling so much right now—a pandemic, a shift in our culture, the effects of systematic racism, and our everyday life circumstances. Faith is all I got! That tiny seed is under constant pressure to grow. I'll get back to UH in a minute, but first I want to share one of my most recent testimonies with you.

On August 10, 2020, I was traveling home from a doctor's appointment when I became the victim of road rage. Keep in mind that a lot of great things had been manifesting in my life at a rapid pace, including the opportunity to write this book with three brilliant women. I live in Houston, Texas. The route from the doctor's office is about a forty-five minute drive to my home. It was around 4:45 p.m. when I made a turn onto the feeder in an attempt to enter the freeway. My path was clear, but suddenly a car came racing up behind me. My attempt to get on the freeway was almost missed now that this driver was tailing me. I refused to let the driver force me out of the way. I proceeded to enter the freeway, but I didn't pick up the additional speed the driver was trying to force me to do. I was already driving over the speed limit. Once we got on the freeway, he pulled up to my driver's side, rolled down his window, brandished a semiautomatic weapon at my face, and fired it. The bullet struck my car in the blind side between the windshield and the driver's window. The coward shot at me and then sped away. Things happened so rapidly I didn't get his license plate. I did call 911, and the dispatcher talked to me, instructing me not to follow and find a safe place to exit the freeway. I followed his instructions and exited the freeway. Once I came to a safe stopping point, I got out of the vehicle and observed that the bullet had indeed hit my car. A terror swept over me, and I began to weep uncontrollably. The dispatcher asked if I was OK. No, I wasn't OK! Someone had just been so enraged while driving that they attempted to murder me in broad daylight on the interstate.

I was shaken. When I left my home that day, I never imagined my safety would be compromised. I know that the devil doesn't like me, but up until that moment, I never thought he would go to that extreme to stop me from existing on this earth. Oh, but he did. He tried it, and I would be remiss if I didn't acknowledge the protection of my God on my life. My journey could have ended that day if it were not for the goodness of God. All of my plans could have been cut short, but I am grateful that He didn't let that happen. My purpose in sharing that testimony is to remind you that no matter how much you train and prepare yourself, you still need someone who is looking out for you and fighting the battles you cannot see. Cover everything in prayer. Pray for yourself, pray for your family, and pray for others. I had a strong sense that my eldest son had been praying for me. He confirmed it that evening when I made it home to my family. The power of prayer can't be compared to anything else. When you pray, pray without doubting. My prayers begin with thanks. I don't ask for anything before I say thank you. The devil tried to take my life and steal my family's and friends' peace.

Now that gave me a new trauma to deal with, but the outpouring of love from many of the people who I know and care about was a bridge to help me heal. Praying, meditating, forgiving, and journaling have been my solace. This is more fuel for my fire. My life's assignment is necessary, and so are the assignments of the people I'm divinely connected to. Our connection is divine. This book was already on the agenda prior to this incident. How powerful is that? The thought that you are so important to the Creator that He would protect my life to be part of getting you a message you need to read. Find what you need in these words. Don't allow what you are hearing on the inside to fall on deaf ears. You have the faith, and you also have to do the work. Faith without works is dead (James 2:14–26; read the AMP version). Imagine what will happen to your dream if you nothing to fulfill it. *Nothing.* Nothing will happen until you combine your faith and your work. This leads me back to UH.

My faith and work are producing good fruit. Acknowledging that is training—training myself to be OK with resting in the idea of me actually accomplishing my goals. We shouldn't think of ourselves more highly than we should, but that does not many we shouldn't think highly of ourselves. Low thinking produces low living. Elevating our thinking is a process, and learning valuable information increases our value. Through higher education, I am accomplishing things I have been dreaming about for years. I believe that my vision board, the images and the Word that I keep before me on a daily basis, are tools that allow me to visualize and build my faith to go back to school at my age. God knows exactly where I need to be. Applying scriptures like Habakkuk 2:2 to my life and the other numerous scriptures that I have shared with you helps light my path. One of my goals is to have sold-out shows in the Hobby Center here in Houston. That is part of the images on my vision board. My obedience to write the vision and make it plain puts me in a position to hear what I need to do next. Since my enrollment, I have had one of my plays produced each semester. That is no easy task, and it is an honor not achieved by all the playwrights in the program. I believe there is favor on my life, but I also know that favor would be nothing if I didn't put in 100 percent commitment. God has worked things out for me so that I am able to maintain employment and be a full-time student. What do you need to work out in your favor so that you can accomplish your dreams? Whatever it is, put your faith in action. Write down what you need. Visualize it happening, and be prepared when the opportunity presents itself.

Currently, one of my full-length plays, *The Carrier*, is in the process of being produced by the university. The opportunity I wanted to network with other people who are passionate about this work has opened to me. Prior to this, I generally stayed to myself on my side of town, doing my work. The few encounters I had trying to network with other artists in this arena had been heartbreaking. Integrity is of the essence, and I know that keeping my word when others have gone back on theirs has been an insulator to keep the river of possibilities flowing my way. You cannot be hooked up with everybody. It is so important in every area of our lives to seek divine connections and maintain our integrity.

The decision to attend UH meant sacrificing driving an hour across town every day. My job is twenty minutes from my house, and I am able to work from home. This moved me way out of my comfort zone, but I prayed and asked God to help me remain faithful and committed. I have, and He has not let me down one bit. Diversity was one of the reasons I sought out attending UH, and once I entered the program, I was surprised by the lack of diversity in the student body and the program. The funny thing is I'm now watching that change right before my eyes, due to the civil unrest after the atrocity of George Floyd's murder that flooded the world. That travesty shined a light in a lot of dark places, including the theatre world. My play will be the first senior-written new work produced at the University of Houston's School of Theatre and Dance with a completely BIPOC cast, playwright, director and dramaturgy team. God has positioned me and the people working with me to make history!

The training that I am undergoing here is so vast. It is teaching me to humble, to be patient, to love and work with all people, to stay committed, and to own my space in the world. It is OK to fill up a room, and it is OK to walk in greatness. Don't make excuses for being unstoppable. That is what you are promised if you are a believer. No matter the trials and tribulations you face, you are more than a conqueror through the Creator's love. Knowing who loves us is half the battle we have to face. If it were not for God's love, I don't know where I would be. That's on the serious.

You may not know when your moment will arrive, but know that it is coming as you prepare for it. Look forward to many moments. Never stop accomplishing and growing. People who stop become stagnant. A triathlon is difficult work, but keep training for it—spirit, mind, and body. We can't quit after one achievement. If we fall short, that is ammunition we need to get back up and keep going. I fell off of my fitness journey, but I am back on. I did not put on all the weight I once had, but the sixty pounds I did put back on are no longer welcome. Sometimes we have to recommit to our goals. This is one of those times for me. How will I get to where I want to be physically? I did what I know works. I wrote the vision out and gave myself a visual goal. So far, I've lost elven pounds. More importantly, I'm getting active again. I reached out to my girlfriends to be accountability partners, purchased a new Fitbit, and am actively changing my eating habits back to what I know works for me.

My purpose is the main driver behind my decision to get on track with my fitness goals. This is my goal: "To consistently live a healthy, active, and fit lifestyle. To remain medication-free. To live a long, satisfied life with a youthful glow and a fit body." To accomplish this goal, I made a plan:

1. Visualize and meditate on my goal every day.
2. Work out at least three days each week—Monday, Wednesday, Friday.
3. Drink at least seven bottles of water daily (120 oz).

4. Do one fun fitness activity each month.
5. Control my portion sizes.
6. Eat more frequently.
7. Eat only fresh/clean snacks.
8. Get more sleep (at least six to seven hours daily).

I can't expect other people to motivate me. Seeking out motivation is my responsibility. On social media, I purposely follow people who are accomplishing their health and fitness goals. This provides inspiration when I need it. I posted my visual and written goal on my bathroom mirror, on the dashboard in my car, and in my office. This is the reminder I need to encourage me to keep pressing toward the mark. Giving up on myself is not an option. My motives for getting on track are pure. I want to practice what I preach in every area of my life.

Create space for yourself. Carve out a spot for you to dream and to work on your goals. Life circumstances can come in and snatch up what you want if you continue to allow them to. We have to fight back. We have to stand our ground. My family and friends have needs, but I can't allow their needs to take a front seat in my life. I firmly believe when I take care of myself, I can take care of others. People have a way of demanding what they want from you regardless of what you have planned. Speak up for yourself. Let them know: "This is what I am doing right now, and this is how I can help you." There may be times when you can't help them at all. Don't allow people to put you on a guilt trip. You are on a mission, and you can't afford to abort that mission. Do what is best for you according to the plans and dreams you have.

When school is in session, I put everyone on notice. "This is what I am working on, and I will not be available to do everything you want me to do when you want me to do it." It is not easy because sometimes feelings are hurt. You must be loving but firm.

Distractions often come in the form of what other people need at the moment. They want their emergencies to be your emergencies. When I can help, I help, but setting healthy boundaries is a must for me. I am empathetic, and if I don't watch myself, I will be running around putting out everybody's fire while my house burns down. Don't burn down your own house. Charity begins at home. Start with loving on yourself and then share that love.

Let's put things into perspective. We are more than what people see on the outside. Our bodies make up one-third of who we are. We have to take time to nourish, train, and grow all three aspects of our lives—spirit, soul, and body. Balancing all three is an ongoing challenge. If we focus on one thing at a time, it will have a domino effect and spill over into other areas of our lives. Whatever traumas you have gone through in the past or present need to be dealt with. Suppressing trauma is unhealthy and can lead you down a self-destructive path. The attacks that you face are designed to rob you of your purpose, but the Creator gave you that purpose, so it is your duty to pursue it. Don't allow it to lie dormant.

Start seeking, asking, and knocking. The answers and the direction you need are only an ask, seek, or knock away. Once you have your answer, it is your job to activate your faith and train for the journey ahead. See yourself as a triathlete. You are competing against yourself to be the best you can be. Be better than you were last year, a month ago, the week before, or the other day. You have what it takes to succeed, no matter how old you are or where you are on your journey. Enjoy the moments. Focus more on enjoying the process and acknowledging how far you have come instead of how far you have to go. You are greater than ... not less than. The greatest that is on the inside of you is not just for you. It is designed to help others. You have to take care of yourself first. If you crash and burn, you won't be good for anything or anyone. Seek out counseling to deal with the things that are hurting or haunting you. No one can tell you how relevant or irrelevant your pain and struggles have been. Your spirit knows. Your spirit wants to guide you toward a place of healing. I believe that healing is found through our Creator. He knows exactly what we need. When we think on good things, we can manifest good things. What we think about ourselves is more powerful than what anyone else says or thinks.

It's time to write out some positivity about who you are. Focus on that, and it will increase. You have a dream. It is time to match that dream with a vision and goals. When you write out what you want and visualize it, you allow yourself to see the bigger picture. Create a vision board. Write out your plans. Make some goals to accomplish those plans. Never compare yourself to others. We all share the human experience, but you are a unique individual. It is important to surround yourself with positive, like-minded people. Changes will start to happen in your life as you ask, seek, and knock. Most of those changes will require you to leave your comfort zone. (One of my favorite books, *The Dream Giver* by Bruce Wilkinson, helped me to understand this better.)

Educate yourself. Whether you read books, do research online, go back to college, or read your Bible, true growth won't happen until you feed yourself the right things. Mentors are essential. Find someone you can look up to for inspiration. One word from them can transform your life. One of my mentors, Helen Callier, said a few words that became engrained on my heart. She said, "Step your game up." I got reenrolled in school after she told me that. It is still a reference point for me when I need a boost. My mother, Pamela Randolph, is one of my great mentors. She told me to dream big. My dreams have expanded because I took her words to heart.

Take the words in this book to heart. Think about them. Talk about them with people you know will encourage you, not coddle you. Do your part to make your dreams a reality. One of my male mentors, Albert Jennings Sr., told me, "Be a producer and not a consumer." He told me that years ago, and it has never left my mind. I started changing my spending habits. Doing something as simple as paying all my bills when or before they are due changed my life. It helped me get my priorities straight. My mentor Dr. Robert Shimko told me, "Write what you know." That has helped me develop my playwriting voice. My father, Patrick T. Randolph, told me, "God is faithful." I believe that, and I can say God has been faithful to me through it all.

Connecting the dots and picking up the clues that your spirit is communicating with you is constant work. There have been times when I missed it, times when I was receiving a definite warning about a person or a situation and I ignored it. One of the things my spirit does is convict me about my own behavior. It is necessary to yield my spirit to the Spirit to receive the correction and guidance that I need. When I resist that correction and guidance, I swear I end up in the dumbest situations—the kind of situations that serve self-destructive, counterproductive behavior. The guard I have for that is the Word, which tells me to guard my heart with all diligence because out of my heart flows my life issues (Proverbs 4:23). What we allow to take root in our hearts will definitely show up in our lives, whether it is good or bad.

Do the work. Get busy doing good things for yourself. I don't mean spa treatments and vacations, although I do mean spa treatments and vacations. First and foremost, I mean get busy doing the work that you are supposed to be doing. Do the things that are necessary for you to make a difference in this world. This is one of my favorite scriptures: "For we are God's handiwork, created in Christ Jesus to do good works, which God prepared in advance for us to do" (Ephesians 2:10 NIV). I recommend reading the verses before that also. My point here is that we have been created to do something by God, and we have to get busy doing it. We are not

God's afterthought. No matter where you are or where you're from, there is some good for you to do.

Remember, no matter how well you train and how prepared you are, you still need someone fighting in your corner, defending you from the evil that you cannot see. Cover yourself in prayer. If you don't know how to pray, ask someone who does to pray for you. Learn how to pray. Learn what to pray. Pray all the time.

Be grateful. The greatest gift you can give back to the Creator is a thankful heart. Find something to be grateful for even in the midst of the wilderness. The wilderness is only temporary. You can thank your way through the wilderness. Appreciation goes a lot further than complaining. You can delay your own blessings with a bad attitude. Your attitude is a reflection of your spirit. Write down what you are grateful for. It can be the smallest thing. Right now, I am grateful for you and the opportunity to be vulnerable with you and share some of the things I am learning.

Learning is an ongoing process, and when we think we have arrived, there is still more room for growth. Acknowledge your accomplishments, but don't get stuck talking about a victory you had twenty years ago. It is the season for new victories. It is the season for new discoveries. It is time for your to reinvent yourself. You can do whatever you set your mind to do, because no matter what you are up against, you have to power to *be courageous anyway!* Take your courage and go conquer something that you have been putting on the back burner. We are in this together. It is all about US! Unity and strength. When you accomplish a goal, let me know about it. I want to celebrate you. You cheer for me, and I cheer for you. We were both born to win this race, and there is absolutely nothing too hard for us because there is nothing too hard for God.

PART 4
But What Did God Say?

MY LIFE, MY JOURNEY

I am Felishia Brown, owner and creator of Maximized Motions and Beastra Athletic Wear. I am a mother of three and grandmother of five. I am fifty and fit. I am divorced but currently restoring the relationship with my ex-husband. It's not easy, but we are working hard to start anew. I am a NASM-certified personal trainer who helps middle-aged women reduce stress and build confidence, and I also work with athletic children to increase athletic performance and prevent injury on and off the court, field, and dance floor through high-intensity interval training. My purpose is to get you to move your body. I also have been teaching in the children's ministry at Praise Christian Center World Outreach for the past fifteen-plus years.

Ever since I can remember, I was always getting people to get up and dance. Even before I became a personal trainer, I would encourage my coworkers to get up and move. I would encourage them to use the stairs instead of the elevator, eat earlier so they could walk during lunch, and drink water instead of soda.

I chose the path of health and fitness because I've always liked to work out. I can remember being in my early twenties. When we would go to the club, my friends would tell me, "Girl, sit down. You're making me tired." I would dance to every song, with or without a partner. I did not care. I was doing what I loved to do—dance. Fast-forward to my forties, and I rejoined the praise dance team at my church. I hadn't danced for extended periods of time in about five years. When we performed our first song, I could barely breathe and almost passed out. I was out of shape, and I needed to do something about it. How could I dance for God and barely make it through a dance? Not long after that, I was invited to a Zumba class. I loved to dance and didn't hesitate to go. Zumba is an interval dance workout. The classes move between high- and low-intensity dance moves designed to get your heart rate up and boost cardio endurance. During that class, mostly Latin music was played, but then the instructor played a hip-hop song, "Booty Wurk" by T-Pain, and I was hooked. In my opinion, that song was the highlight of the class. It was during this class I had the epiphany of what I wanted to do for the rest of my life. I had so much fun that I decided on the spot I wanted to become a Zumba instructor. I could see myself dancing into my old age, so why not do this for a living? A couple of months later, I became a Zumba instructor. I had been given a piece of the puzzle, and the path to my destiny and purpose had now been discovered. After joining the gym where I took the Zumba classes, I began working out with weights. I liked the way lifting weights made me feel, like a beast. My confidence level skyrocketed. I didn't know at the time, but physical activity releases hormones called endorphins, which minimizes discomfort and serotonin, which makes you happy. (They are sometimes called the happy hormones.) Anyway, it took my mind off of what I had going on at the moment.

When my workout was complete, my problems didn't seem as big or would disappear altogether.

THE STARTING POINT: MY WHY

I became a personal trainer because I wanted to use my story, my life, and my why to help other women gain confidence—the same confidence I received when I worked out. I went through a divorce, and it was painful and stressful, and I was depressed. I lost about thirty pounds. I had no desire to eat, so I starved myself and lost weight. I prayed and asked God to help me make me a better me. I wanted to be better, not bitter. I believe God answered my prayers with Zumba and free weightlifting (the use of dumbbells). Thus, I quickly learned how to physically deal with stress: I worked out. I later learned physical exercise can be used as a substitute to metabolize the excessive stress hormones and restore your body and mind to a calmer, more relaxed state. God is so amazing to create our bodies in such a way that when physical activity is increased, stress is reduced and our energy and confidence level are increased.

We were created to move. Here are some additional benefits to exercising to get you motivated to increase your physical activity:

1. It will increase your energy levels by improving the state of your cardiovascular system.
2. It increases muscular strength and reduces joint and lower back pain.
3. It helps you maintain a healthy weight and induces weight loss.
4. It reduces LDL cholesterol, which can clog your arteries, and increases HDL cholesterol, also known as good cholesterol.
5. It lowers the risk of type 2 diabetes, controlling blood sugar levels.

6. It enhances the immune system by increasing the blood flow, which carries oxygen and good bacteria throughout the body.
7. It also reduces the chance of you developing osteoporosis.
8. It boosts self-esteem and confidence.
9. It increases mental clarity.
10. It decreases fat while increasing lean muscle mass.

When was the last time you worked out? If it's been more than two weeks, you'd better get off the couch and do something—now. Becoming physically active is not hard to do. You have to decide when and what you want to do. There are a variety of group classes available; cycling, Zumba, Soul Grooves, yoga, hot yoga, strength conditioning, pole classes, and hip-hop class are a few of my favorites. Get with a group of friends. They will keep you motivated and hold you accountable. If you can afford it, get a personal trainer. If this is all too much, begin by taking walks in your neighborhood. Find a nice park with a trail or a school nearby. Small steps lead to big changes. Be consistent. Actions require consistency in order for the changes to last. Also, it wouldn't hurt to get a new mindset about physical activity.

Here are a few affirmations/declarations to say out loud to help you start thinking positively about your fitness journey:

1. My mind is focused, and I am ready to get in shape.
2. My body is strong; no exercise is too hard for me.
3. I love working out.
4. I am excited about my fitness journey.
5. I have a strong body and mind.
6. I am transforming my body into a more fit and healthier me.
7. Every day, I am losing weight, reducing stress, and becoming stronger mentally, emotionally, and physically.

8. I take care of my body the best way I know how.
9. I am capable of achieving any health and fitness goal I set.
10. I love the way I feel after I work out.
11. I love my body, and my body loves the way I take care of it.
12. Self-care is a must for me.
13. I am fully committed to my workouts.
14. I deserve to be healthy and fit.
15. My body was created to be fit and functional.
16. My purpose requires me to be in the best shape possible.
17. I will live a long, fit, and healthy lifestyle.

Enoch walked with God (Genesis 5:22); Noah walked with God (Genesis 6:9).

In the Bible, they walked almost everywhere they went. Adam and Eve walked in the Garden of Eden—and in the cool of the day, I might add. Others walked in the wilderness. They walked by the riverside, they walked in the field, they walked upon the dry land in the midst of the sea. They walked all night through the plains and passed over the Jordan River. You get the picture: they walked.

Here are some benefits of walking to get you motivated to walk:

- improves circulation
- changes your mood
- clears your head
- improves sleep
- reduces loss of bone mass
- helps you lose weight
- strengthens your muscles
- improves your breathing
- reduces risks of dementia and Alzheimer's disease
- allows for time for planning

Anyway, the Bible mentions Noah and Enoch walked with God. It probably means living a righteous life. Doing things God's way. Enoch walked with God and was no more. He did not die a physical death. I was worn out by my last job. I was working twelve-plus hours a day and sometimes on the weekend. The money was very good, but I didn't have peace in my life. Time and again, I would encounter the same pattern where I didn't like a person and/or they didn't like me for the same reasons: I was good at what I did, and the leader in me would make suggestions to change a process or procedure, and someone somewhere took it as me trying to take over their job. Deep down, I knew God wanted me to get back to doing health and fitness. But I was stubborn because I didn't see how I could pay my bills without working. I didn't have the entrepreneur mindset I have now. As mentioned earlier, I became a Zumba instructor, but it wasn't moving as quickly as I wanted it to, so I let it go and returned to my comfort zone, logistics. I had been doing air logistics for almost twenty-two years, transporting deep-sea drilling rig parts overseas by air, and in my regulate intro voice, "I was damn good at it too." Nevertheless, I was unhappy even though the money was good. I called up a good friend of mine, and she had no problem telling me I needed to talk to God.

I remember getting up the next morning and taking a walk. Upon entering the track, I heard my Prophet say, "Write down what you hear." So I put on my praise and worship, opened notes on my phone, and went for a much-needed walk. I remember God giving me instructions. I had peace about quitting my job and going into personal training full-time. I had it all planned out. I was going to leave my job at the end of the year and live off of my 401(k) until I could make it as a personal trainer. But God had different plans, and I was fired on October 18, 2018. I enrolled in NASM's personal training certification course and became a certified personal trainer in April 2019. After looking back on the last two years, I didn't do too badly. I work one-fourth of the hours, get to spend much more time with the grandkids, moved into a new house, and have a new car (not spanking brand-new but new to me). I can honestly say I've done all right. God has seen me through the last two years without big corporation money. It was taking a walk with God that resurrected my dreams and passion for health and fitness. I have to wonder, how many people who will read this book need their dreams and aspirations resurrected? I encourage you to take a walk the very next chance you get.

The Bible encourages you to write: write the vision; write in a book the words I say unto you; write the words of this song; record this and record that.

Back to me reducing stress. Journaling helped me. I can't recall how many journals I filled up when going through my divorce, but I can say I threw away crates full of them as a way of letting go of the hurt caused by my divorce. I filled up journals with my emotions, my workouts, my conversations with God, my conversations with family, friends, and coworkers, my conversations with my ex-husband and, at that time, his new wife. Whatever I went through that day went in my journals. No matter how good, bad, or ugly, I wrote it down; it was my release. If you don't journal, I encourage you to begin today, especially if you are the type of person who easily goes off on people. Before you fly off the handle the next time, try writing out what you're going to say exactly the way you would say it. Then read it out loud to yourself, but pretend you are the other person. Is what you said justified? Does it tear down the other person? Will you get them to change a behavior by your words and current tone? Can you say what you said in a softer tone? Can you use softer words and still make the same point? Journaling also allows you to see you, to check yourself before you wreck yourself, so to speak. Here are some other benefits of journaling:

- It helps manage anxiety.
- It reduces stress.
- It helps cope with depression.
- It can help you prioritize your fears, problems, and concerns.
- You'll learn ways to control them by recognizing what triggers them.

Below are some tips for journaling:

- Write every day, several times a day if needed.
- When you can't write in a journal, type out your thoughts on your phone or your computer for you to transfer later.
- When you can't write, do a voice recording and transfer it later.
- Write whatever you feel like writing; it's your journal, and no one needs to know what you've written unless you choose to share.

"At the end of ten days it was seen that they were better in appearance and fatter in flesh than all the youths who ate the king's food" (Daniel 1:15). You are what you eat. Our bodies were also created to repair themselves, but they have to get the nutrients needed for such repair. The nutrients are found in the food you eat and are essential for the recovery stage after you work out but are also essential for normal repair. If you are not getting the nutrients your body needs, your body cannot function or recover properly. It is like driving your car and not putting fuel in it. If you don't fuel up, you don't get very far. You do preventative maintenance on your car too, right? Oil changes, regular tune-ups, rotating tires, and replacing filters help to keep the vehicle running properly. In the same sense, you have to do things for your body to keep it running properly. Eating right and physical activity are your preventative maintenance. Eating properly doesn't mean going vegan, but it does mean eating the proper amounts of carbohydrates, protein, and fats, spread out over five to seven meals per day, from healthy, nutrient-rich foods providing other essential nutrients like vitamins and minerals. Maintaining adequate fluid intake is also vital. You should drink at least half your weight in ounces of water. For example, if you weigh one hundred pounds, you should drink at least fifty ounces of water daily. Eating properly on a regular basis can do the following:

- improve general health and fitness
- help to build muscle mass
- help to lose fat
- help to reduce fatigue
- improve stamina
- improve tissue repair
- improve mental focus
- improve strength
- improve immune system
- improve sleep

You want to keep up the preventative maintenance on your body by exercising and eating right so you can do everyday normal things like chasing after kids, going to work, cleaning up, cooking, or just having fun.

Quick story: I was a junk-a-holic. I worked for a company that landed a large short-term contract. The bid was going out between us and two other companies. It was a major contract for our company, and we had to do everything in our power to keep the business. That meant working extra hours and days to win the bid. More hours worked meant less time cooking for me and my family. Thus, I would grab quick snacks at work, and the vending machines became my chef. My everyday breakfast was chili and cheese Fritos, A&W

Root Beer soda, and Snickers (the not-going-anywhere-for-a-while candy bar). Anyway, I ate a lot of junk and processed food because I didn't have time to cook. I did this for years until I took a nutrition class at my church. I learned your poop wasn't supposed to stink. This statement confounded my brain. My poop had always stunk, and so did my gas. After the class, I set up a consultation with the nutritionist and learned about the colon. She showed me a picture of a healthy colon versus an unhealthy colon. The healthy colon was pink and wrinkled but neat, and the unhealthy colon was black, green, and clogged. It was as if I could smell that unhealthy colon through the picture. It was gross and made me want to throw up. Just thinking about it makes me gag. Anyway, that was definitely a crowning conversation moment. I wanted to clean my colon and keep it clean. Thus, I began my journey of eating healthy. Do I stick to it 100 percent of the time? Heavens no. It's a journey in itself, but I will get there.

Here are some small steps to eating healthier, things I practice faithfully:

- Drink water instead of soda. It was the first thing I cut out of my diet.
- Eat more fruit. I buy fruit and cut it up and make a big fruit bowl. Bananas and apples make a quick morning snack.
- Keep healthy food readily available. I buy more individually packed healthy snacks, which is awesome if you're a person always on the go.
- Use whole grain flour in baking recipes.
- Use brown rice over white rice or cut out rice altogether and try quinoa or cauliflower rice (don't knock it until you try it).
- Eat more nuts.

> I am marvelously made! … what a creation … I was sculpted from nothing into something. (Psalm 149:14–16)

> For no man ever yet hated his own flesh; but nourisheth and cherisheth it. (Ephesians 5:29)

I can recall a time when I wasn't happy with my body. I thought I had to be thick to be loved. I wanted badly to gain weight to be what I thought was the ideal woman. There wasn't anything wrong with the way I was, but I wanted to be thick. Anyway, I didn't gain weight on purpose. I gained weight after having three children. Contrary to what they say in the magazines, men love thick women. You don't have to believe me. Take a poll on social media and ask one hundred men which they prefer. You'd be amazed at what you find out. Anyway, along with the thickness came a juicy booty and all the attention a girl with low self-esteem would ever want or need—more attention than I could handle or was used to getting. Too much of something can make you sick. And that is what I became, sick. Sick of the attention, sick of the arguments I was having because of my newfound attention and my new way of dressing. I was getting all the attention from the fellas, and now, just like in high school, I was being hated by the ladies. I quickly discovered I didn't like the attention I was getting. I wanted badly to be thin again. I tried changing the way I ate. I went on what I thought was a good diet— the Subway diet. I ate Subway every day because that's how Jared lost weight. Remember Jared the Subway guy? Anyway, I did lose some weight, but I was still unhealthy. Now fast-forward to after my divorce. I became skinny. Size 2 skinny. As I stated before, my divorce was painful, and I went into a state of depression. That's when the journaling came into play. Anyway, I was still unhappy with my body. I had to fall in love with me no matter what size I was. I didn't want to care about what other people thought of how I looked. I didn't want to do it for them; I wanted to do it for me.

I realized, thick or thin, I had to realize God made me unique. I am fearfully and wonderfully made. I am an amazing creation, and so are you. If you don't love you, you'll open yourself up for others to misuse and abuse you. When you realize God made an amazing creation, a piece of valuable art, you'll begin loving yourself, believing in yourself, trusting yourself, and caring for yourself—mind, body, and soul. We let what other people feel or think about us dictate how we feel about ourselves. We let fashion magazines tell us we should all be a perfect size 4, when that is not the case. It shouldn't matter what or how others feel about you; it only matters how you feel about you. Focus on the positives, and the negatives will soon disappear or at least become less important.

The Bible says to cast down imaginations and every high thing that exalts itself against the knowledge of God. This means replace negative thoughts in your head with positive and factual thoughts from God. This is exactly what I did. I found out what God says about me and began to say the same thing. Just what is God saying about you? Google "what does the Bible say about self-confidence." You will find hundreds of scriptures about what God has to say about you. I picked two to talk about: Psalm 139:14 and Ephesians 5:26 to begin with. I have listed several versions so we can get a better understanding of what God is trying to say to us. Read each one of the statements out loud. See yourself as God sees you.

Psalm 139:14

> I will praise thee; for I am fearfully and wonderfully made: marvelous are thy works; and that my soul knoweth right well. (KJV)

I will give thanks *and* praise to You, for I am fearfully and wonderfully made; Wonderful are Your works, And my soul knows it very well. (AMP)

Oh yes, you shaped me first inside, then out; you formed me in my mother's womb. I thank you, High God-you're, breathtaking! Body and soul, I am marvelously made! I worship in adoration—what a creation! You know me inside and out, you know every bone in my body; You know exactly how I was made, bit by bit, how I was sculpted from nothing into something. Like an open book, you watched me grow from conception to birth; all the stages of my life were spread out before you, The days of my life all prepared before I'd even lived one day. (MSG)

Ephesians 5:29

No one abuses his own body, does he? No, he feeds and pampers it. (MSG)

For no one ever hated his own body, but [instead] he nourishes *and* protects and cherishes it. (AMP)

No one ever hated his own body. Instead, he feeds and takes care of it, as Christ takes care of the church. (GW)

From the above scriptures, I have made several affirmations or "I am" statements. In order to get rid of the negative thoughts in your head, you must say positive ones out loud. I have learned over the years that what you say matters; you might as well say something positive.

Affirmations:

- Thick or thin, I love the skin I'm in.
- I am fearfully and wonderfully made.
- I am a wonderful work of the Lord my God.
- I am shaped by my Father in heaven.
- I am breathtaking.
- I am a wonderful creation.
- I am made the exact way God intended me to be made.
- I am God's sculpture.
- Mind, body and soul, I am marvelously made.
- I love my body. I feed it well and take care of it well.

"As a man thinketh so is he" (Proverbs 23:7).

The comedian Katt Williams put this in perspective for me in his Pimp Chronicles performance. If you haven't seen it, You-Tube "Katt Williams Self-Esteem." It will change your life. He said (I am paraphrasing for those who can't handle Katt Williams's delivery), "You have to be the shit to you. Don't wait for another person to verify you. Don't let others be in control of your thoughts." He screamed, "It's called *self-esteem*. It's esteem of yourself. You are not supposed to let anyone mess up how you feel about you. You have to get in control of your thoughts of you." His point of view made it clear to me I had to learn how to control and change my thoughts. I had to learn true self-esteem. I had to be the shit to me. This brings me to self-talk. I had to have conversations with myself. Michael Jackson said it best: "I'm talking to the man in the mirror. I'm asking him to change his ways."

"But David encouraged himself in the Lord his God" (1 Samuel 30:6).

Self-talk is powerful. David strengthened, encouraged, and talked to himself. I am not forgetting the fact he did it in the Lord, but so many times, we call on people to pick us up out of a funk, and we are more than able to do the job ourselves. I told myself I would be better and not bitter after my divorce. This was my actual declaration: "I will be better, not bitter." I must have said it a million times. I told myself I would be better and not bitter. I prayed and asked God to help me be better and not bitter. This put me on a road that led me to take every self-development class I could find. I learned about affirmations and how powerful they are. Start with these I found on the internet, fifty-five positive self-esteem affirmations from www.wildsimplejoy.com:

- I am whole just as I am.
- I give myself unconditional love!
- I feel great about who I am.
- My life is amazing!
- I have unlimited power.
- I believe in myself and my power.
- Others love me for who I am.
- I treat myself with respect and honor.
- People treat me with respect.
- I view myself through kind eyes.
- I feel comfortable speaking my mind.
- I love to share my ideas and thoughts.
- I have unique and special ideas to share with the world.
- I am grateful for the amazing, wonderful things in my life!
- I deserve everything I desire.
- My life is rewarding and filled with joy.
- I am blessed.

- My life is full of adventure and incredible experiences.
- I accept and embrace myself for who I am.
- I love who I am inside and out.
- I am creative and flexible, and I go with the flow of life.
- I expect the best for myself!
- My life is abundant.
- The Universe is generous with health, joy, and abundance!
- I learn and grow every day.
- I adapt and change to my circumstances. I flow like a river.
- I am worthy of all the abundance, love, and amazing experiences I want.
- Others look up to me.
- I feel joyful to look at how far I've come.
- I appreciate all the lessons that life has taught me.
- I grow and become a better version of myself every day!
- I am confident and intelligent.
- I am beautiful.
- I love myself more and more each passing day.
- I appreciate me.
- I give praise to myself and others naturally and effortlessly!
- I naturally feel good about myself!
- I forgive myself.
- I easily forgive others.
- I do my best every day.
- I am optimistic and positive!
- I am courageous and outgoing!
- I fearlessly follow my dreams!
- I am capable of achieving everything I want.
- Others value my skills and knowledge.
- I contribute my ideas and thoughts easily.
- My life is a blessing.
- I am loved.

- I love myself. I accept myself. I forgive myself.
- I know myself and I honor my boundaries.
- I radiate self-confidence!
- I have great potential that I tap into every day!
- I can achieve anything I put my mind to.
- I make a difference in the world.

Also begin teaching your children about self-esteem. Read *Chrysanthemum* by Kevin Henkes. *Chrysanthemum* is a funny and honest school story about teasing, self-esteem, and acceptance. I read this children's book as a college student, and it had a tremendous impact on me.

THE LAP—THE LONG PART OF THE JOURNEY

"Faith without works is dead" (James 2:26).

One part of change is taking action. Just doing it. Whatever it is. Sometimes the start of something is the hardest thing to do, but once you begin, everything begins to flow. Let's talk about increasing your physical activity. What if I don't like to work out? Or what if I just don't want to work out? And here is my favorite: I don't have the energy for any kind of physical activity. Well, duh, you don't have energy because you don't move your body enough and/or you are not eating right. So how do we get our bodies moving? That is the million-dollar question. If you are a person who likes to put things off, and we all do it at some point in our lives, you have to decide to get the Nike mindset, "Just do it." Stop procrastinating, stop making excuses, get up off your booty, and just do it. I used to be a procrastinator. I always had time to do it tomorrow; I never had time to do it today. Truth be told, I just didn't want to do it today. I prayed and asked God to help me overcome procrastination. I needed Him to help me stop making excuses. I needed Him to help me to stop being lazy. You may find it strange or even funny, but I couldn't do this on my own. I wanted to become a person of action, and the following statement helped me: you have to crawl before you walk.

Crawling

Start by getting out of bed and stretching. Stretch before you go to work. I used to work with a lady who, every morning, got out of her car and stretched for about five minutes before she came into the building. I asked her why she stretched before work. She said it helped her reduce stress before it started. She was the calmest person I've ever worked with. I don't care what we had going on; she was unbothered. You may think five minutes is not a long time; what good would that do? You'd be amazed at what five minutes of stretching a day can do for your body.

By incorporating five to ten minutes of dynamic and static stretches into your daily routine, you can increase your range of motion, improve your posture, ease your mind, and reduce injury.

Walking

It is OK to walk before you run. I would treat my task as if I were a long-distance runner. I would walk until I got to the point where I could run. We are using walking as a comparison for going slowly, moving in slow motion, or dragging out a task. Let's take something as simple as getting up to go work out. Yes, I love to work out, but getting up and getting there wasn't always easy for me. I used to work out before coming to work, and getting up was the hardest part. I would drag the task out until I got in my truck. For example, I get up, shower, put my clothes on, put on my socks and shoes, brush my teeth, grab my water, and get in my truck. I have listed seven tasks. Let's just say for the sake of simple math it takes me five minutes to do each task. That's thirty-five minutes, slow or not. Doing it slowly, I would take an extra two minutes to do each task. That's forty-nine minutes to get ready. Doing it slowly gave me time to get my mind right. Sometimes, I would have to talk myself into going by saying, "I'm going to work out. I am going to make myself better. I am going to make myself stronger. I am going to be a better me." I did this until I got into my truck.

There are pros and cons to moving slowly. Pro: the job still got done. Con: because it takes longer, sometimes it would cause me to miss out on a class. I only had this happen maybe twice before I began putting a little pep in my step. I remember one time in particular. I arrived at the studio right at 5:00 a.m., and another person arrived seconds before me and just happened to take the last spot in the class. All because I was dragging my ass. That was the last time I did it slowly. I didn't say you'd be doing it slowly forever; I said this was a starting point, getting you to take action. Like walking before running, you have to start somewhere.

Jogging

Jogging is the point between walking and running. Breaking the task up into smaller pieces is in between doing the job slowly (walking) and flat-out getting it done (running). Look at the whole picture. Let's take, for example, cleaning your room. The room is the whole picture. Now let's break up the picture into smaller parts. Each wall would be a part (four parts total), each corner would be a part (four parts total), as would be the dresser, bed, and nightstand. Now we have one picture of the room broken into eleven parts. Clean each part without going back and forth from one part to the next and back to the original part. Create a timeline if needed. Take five to ten minutes to clean each part. Then take a break. Before you know it, your room is clean, and it didn't take as long as you originally thought because you broke it into smaller sections. This can be applied to beginning your workout routine. Maybe you feel like you can't workout one hour a day for three to five days a week. Don't let the hourlong workout scare you. Start by doing fifteen- to thirty-minute sessions per day. Or if you are determined to work out an hour a day but don't have the time, break it up into fifteen- or thirty-minute sessions. Thirty-minute sessions can be done, one in the morning and one in the evening. You can do a fifteen-minute session every three or four hours throughout the day. Just move your body.

Running

Whether you are a marathon runner or sprinter, you come out of the blocks and don't stop until you cross the finish line. Plan it out and get it done. The night before I work out, I select my leggings, the tank, the panties and bra, socks, and tennis shoes. I put my socks inside my shoes and place them at the foot of the bed (wherever you sit to put your shoes on is where you need to place them). I put my leggings, tank, panties, and bra on a hanger over the bathroom door or the doorknob. This is called wardrobe planning, where you select your clothes the night before. I select the bath towel and dry-off towels and put them on the sink. I place my deodorant and lotion next to the towels. I am all set. I don't have to think about anything in the morning; everything is ready to go. And it almost guarantees I will work out because it would be a waste of time to select clothes the night before and not get up and work out. This reduces the stress of deciding what to wear, and it reduces the time it takes to get ready in the morning because I do not have to think about what I am going to wear. I can run through this process. Side note: put your wallet and phone in your purse the night before too. I got up early one morning to go work out, left the house, stopped by the gas station for gas, and discovered I had left my wallet at home. SMH@me.

During your run, don't forget your water breaks. This is where you take your power naps or time to relax. And if you are also like me, you need your power naps.

By the way, benefits of power naps (me time) follow:

- improve productivity
- increase creativity
- boost alertness
- lift your spirits

"Lord, teach us to pray" (Luke 11:1)

I would be lying if I said I made it through my life without prayer. Prayers don't have to be long and eloquent; they need to come from a sincere and humble heart. I pray about everything.

I remember driving to work one day and asking God/Jesus to come and have a seat on the passenger side while I talked to Him. I can still see myself patting the passenger seat as I invited Him into my car. I didn't know it at the time, but I was inviting Him into my heart. I wanted to have a conversation with Him. Moses talked to God. Noah walked and talked to God. Enoch walked and talked with God. I wanted to do the same thing. I didn't know how to pray. I didn't know what to say or how to say it. I didn't even know at the time that I was actually praying. As a child, I had been taught, "Now I lay me down to sleep, I pray the Lord my soul to keep. If I should die before I wake, I pray the Lord my soul to take." I also learned the Lord's Prayer, but I learned to repeat it. I didn't know what I was saying. Yes, I want God to keep my soul. And I wanted my daily bread. Wait—what is daily bread? At the time, I thought it meant physical food. I was probably in my thirties before I understood it to mean His Word and provision. What else can we ask God for?

What else can I talk to Him about? God wants to have a relationship with us. He wants us to give it all to Him. He wants to move on our behalf, so He can get the glory. He wants to load us daily with benefits, our daily bread. He also wants us to ask Him in prayer. *Lord, teach us how to pray. Tell us what to say.* If you don't know how to pray, it's OK. God will take whatever words you use to speak with Him and listen to you. He not only listens to your words, but He listens to your heart.

So how should we pray?

We pray by ...

- *Asking God.* We can ask God to help us with everything. I asked God to help me stop being lazy. I asked Him to help me be better, not bitter. I knew one person who used to ask God daily to help her find clothes to wear. Another person asked God to help her with her bowling game. We can ask God for anything. I am not saying we will get everything we ask for; I am saying this is one way to go to Him.
- *Thanking God.* We should thank God for everything. When Jesus healed the leprous men, only one came back and thanked Him. He asked, "Weren't there ten of you?" The leprous man said yes. Jesus replied, "Then where are the other nine? Only you came back to thank me. Your faith has made you whole." Think about this for a minute. Jesus had already cleansed them, but He made this man whole. What was he lacking in his life for Jesus to make him whole? Maybe he had more than leprosy. Maybe Jesus pulled that thing up from the root, and that made him whole. Isn't that reason enough to be thankful? What are you going through? What healing do you need? What deliverance do

you need? What has God done for you already? Think of something and thank Him for it right now. In some areas of your life, because you are thanking Him, He is making that area whole. He is doing more than just cleansing; it is whole (nothing missing, nothing lacking).

- *Praising God.* Praising God helped bring me out of depression. I would tell God how good He was to me and my kids.
- *Worshipping God.* Worshipping God also helped bring me out of depression. I would tell him how much I loved Him. I would get on my knees and put my face to the floor and show how much I revered Him.
- *Supplication* is a humble and earnest prayer. It is a heartfelt and sincere prayer.
- *Interceding* is praying for someone else. Just do it, even if you consider that person your enemy. God chooses people who are willing to obey. God will tell us to do something we don't know we have the strength to do until we actually do it. He is looking for our obedience. The Word says, "Obedience is better than sacrifice." I remember when God asked me to pray for a person at the time I hated. I will never forget the day God asked me to pray for them. I was watching a Tyler Perry play. The woman in the play was going through hell. I remember seeing the person's face who God asked me to pray for. *Wait, what? You want me to do what? How could you ask me to do such a thing?* Yes, I said this to God. Then God answered: "If you don't pray for them, no one else will." His statement paralyzed me. I remember sitting still and being confused, mad, and amazed all at the same time. *God, you know what the person did to me.* Finally, obedience took me to my prayer closet. It took me almost two hours to let the first words out of my mouth.

God revealed to me this person was hurt and was living a life bound and tormented by darkness. I am not sure if it was true or not; it could have been a tactic to get me to pray. When I was finally able to formulate the words, I prayed, and then I cried. Even though I didn't like it, I didn't want them to go through hell. I didn't know how to pray or what to say. I am not going to lie and say I wanted them blessed. Nevertheless, I would go into my closet, call their name, and ask God to bless them and then pray in the spirit. I found out later that when we intercede on behalf of someone, we ask God to keep them from His wrath. I don't know what my prayers did for them, but I know they were working on my behalf. I was being delivered from the hurt and pain. I got to the point where no matter what happened, it did not bother me. Not soon after that, God changed the whole situation around.

- *Getting straight to the point* is not beating around the bush. Jesus, in the Garden of Gethsemane, asked God to let the cup pass from Him. He went away to check on the disciples, then came back and said again, "If this is the way it has to be, then OK, Your will be done" (Felishia's version). Jesus did not sugarcoat the fact that He did not want to die on the cross. And we can be frank with God as well. Again, He already knows everything, so it is OK to voice our opinion. Just know it is our obedience He is looking for. Might as well do like Jesus and let God's will be done.

- *Calling out to God*. It's OK to call His name out loud. Remember the ten leprous men. Scripture says they lifted their voices and called Jesus's name.

- *Drawing near to God*. The Bible says if we draw near to Him, He will draw near to us.

- *Going to God continually, persistently, never stopping.* One scripture says not to cease in praying. There was an unsaved judge and a woman who went to him consistently, getting on his nerves so much so that he gave the woman what she wanted because she was so persistent.

- *Confessing our sins to God.* Don't just ask God to change someone else. Tell God what you did. He knows all and sees all anyway.

- *Calling upon His name.* Scripture says we should ask everything in the name of Jesus. After my divorce, I prayed, "Jesus, help me." I prayed those three words more than anything else because my pain at the time was unbearable and I didn't know any scriptures that would help me. I could only pray, "Jesus help me." And it worked.

- *Casting* (throwing, tossing, pitching, flinging, or hurling) our burdens (cares, problems, difficulties, troubles) on God. When my feelings are hurt, I cast it on God. I go to God and say, "God, this person hurt my feelings. I am tossing it Your way," and I leave it with Him. If I am being a baby, God will tell me so. But if I am not, God always, 100 percent of the time takes care of them. I'm not talking about hurting them or anything like that, but He will always show them themselves. On a few occasions, I've had people come and apologize to me for something they've said or how they acted. And I never said a word to them. I just gave it all to God.

I must reiterate: your prayers do not have to be eloquent, elaborate prayers. God already knows what you need before you ask. Just do it.

"He healeth the broken in heart, and bindeth up their wounds" (Psalm 147:3).

The season right after my divorce had many crowning

conversations—conversations I will never forget and that I hope inspire and encourage you. It was constant praise, worship, and dance. I did this for hours at a time, until my soul was satisfied. It was a sermon I heard from TD Jakes. I remember him saying this one line in particular, "Let the redeemed of the Lord say, 'So!'" He said the word *so* with so much confidence and so loudly I felt like he was talking directly to me through the tape player. I had another conversation with my apostle, where I was told to stop looking defeated. It made me get my act together. There were countless conversations with a guy who was also going through a divorce and a friend who let me talk to her until I was blue in the face. If she ever reads this book, "Friend, if all I had was a penny to my name, I'd give you half."

I cried so much after my divorce. I felt like a part of my soul was gone. Side note: the way you grew up makes a difference when it comes to marriage. Before you say I do, know the history of the family. It will help you understand your mate and keep you from a lot of heartache. Now, let's break down the journey to my healing.

PRAISE, WORSHIP, AND DANCE

> Then the virgin will rejoice in the dance, And the young men and old, together, For I will turn their mourning into joy And will comfort them and make them rejoice after their sorrow. (Jeremiah 31:13)

Of course, I didn't know this scripture at the time, but this is literally what God did for me. He took away my hurt, anguish, and suffering and turned it all into joy. He comforted me in my time of loneliness. He gave me peace, joy, and laughter. He turned my darkness to light. He gave me hope and encouragement. I knew somehow I would make it. I spent hours dancing, praising, worshipping, and crying to God. When I was done, I would feel fulfilled, full of peace and God's love for me. It was as if God would take my heavy garment off, hold me in His arms, and then give me a lighter garment to put on. I think I praised and worshipped God for at least a year. It didn't happen overnight. Healing is a process and sometimes takes days, months, and, yes, even years. But I made it through the dark time. I wasn't completely healed, but I was to the point I could function and move forward in life. I still had to deal with the junk on the inside of me. I still had unforgiveness inside of me. And to be completely healed, completely free, I had to forgive everyone, including myself.

Receiving a right now Word from God.

> It is the spirit that quickeneth; the flesh profiteth nothing: the words that I speak unto you, they are spirit, and they are life. (John 6:63)

God gave me my life back when I received those words from God. God is all-knowing and knows us inside and out. God knew what I needed to hear, when I needed to hear it, and the way I needed to hear it. I kept repeating those words whenever I heard the enemy whisper in my ear anything negative. I would say out loud, "So." I would talk to the devil and say, "So! Devil, you can't have me. So! You can't have my mind! You can't have my children! You can't have my husband!" I would then feel a sense of victory. When I didn't feel like getting dressed, I would hear in my spirit, "Stop looking defeated." So I would get up and try to at least look the part, even if I didn't feel it on the inside.

HAVING A FRIEND TO LEAN ON

One friend taught me that men cry. Men have feelings and emotions they keep bottled up. Men love hard. Men also wish like hell they knew how to make marriages work. I also learned no matter how much a man tries to replace a true love, they will never be able to do it. They can try through being with multiple women or overindulging in material things. Only God can satisfy their souls.

Another friend taught me how important a father-daughter relationship is. Her relationship with her dad made me talk to my daddy more—not just talk but listen.

I don't wish divorce on anyone, because divorce is painful. If you're going through one, I pray on the other side of it you are better and not bitter.

MAXIMIZED LIFE BIBLE INSTITUTE

I also attended Bible college, which had the most impact on my journey through divorce. It brought me closer to God and made me more sensitive to His voice. It made me obedient. When I started Bible college, I didn't have a car. I rode the bus to work. I would get off, and if I did not have a ride, I would have to walk from the bus stop to church, which is about three and a half miles and took me a little over an hour. I can say the prayer class had the biggest impact on my life—so much so that after I graduated, I taught the prayer class.

During prayer class, we were giving an assignment to pray in the spirit for ten minutes each day and journal what happened. Praying in the spirit and journaling helped me to focus on God and brought me out of my depression. It helped me take my focus off of what was going on in my life and focus on God. I realized I needed to focus on God. God is a jealous God, and we are not to worship any gods before Him. Attending MLBTI helped me get my life together. It kept me from making crazy decisions that would have sent me spiraling on a downward path. Here are just a few things that happened because of MLBTI:

- I received clear and specific instructions from God. It helped me to know who to date and who not to date.
- Praying in the spirit helped me get organized.
- I received wisdom for my children.
- I learned how to forgive and let go.
- I received wisdom for my ex-husband.
- I was forced to look at myself. I was at a low point in my life and needed to see myself as God saw me. I was forced to put myself in check.
- I saw my kids' future.
- I was told to make a list of things I desired. I wanted a car without a car note. One day while in prayer at church, I received a Toyota Camry, and just like that, I had a car without a car note.

I will open the windows of heaven for you and pour out a blessing so great you won't have room enough to receive it. (Malachi 3:10)

Paying my tithes. I pray Malachi 3:10–11 over my tithes. Here is my exact prayer/declaration: "I pay my tithes. He will open up the windows of heaven and pour me out a blessing that there shall not be room enough for me to receive it. God will pour out blessings beyond my wildest dreams. He will defend me against marauders and protect my wheat fields and vegetable gardens against plunderers."

All my classes are filled with twenty-one or more people. People are lined up to get into my classes. People all over are looking for me. They are looking for my energy, my personality and my wisdom. I have studied and have no reason to be ashamed. I am accurately and skillfully coaching: technique, form and transformation on the treadmill, rowers, and the strength floor. Now I have regulars in my classes. I love the community/family vibe that is built around my classes. God surely opened the windows of heaven for me.

LOVE IS ...

From high school up to my early twenties, maybe twenty-two or twenty-three, I was promiscuous. I must admit I was young and dumb. I didn't know what real love was. All I knew was the boys loved me, or so I thought. They just loved the sex. I said earlier if you don't have self-love, you allow others to misuse you. And if you don't know what love is, there is no way to begin to speak about self-love. I didn't know how to love myself. You don't know what you don't know. When I was young, no one sat me down and talked with me about sex. What I knew about sex I had learned from my friends. And they were all having sex, so I thought that's what I was supposed to do too. I didn't know what love was, how to give it or how to receive it.

When I was married, I thought sex was showing love. I didn't know I needed love and affection. I remember reading 1 Corinthians 13. I found out what true love was and why I wasn't getting what I needed or deserved. I needed affection and affirmation. Jealousy isn't love. Buying me stuff isn't love. Having sex with me isn't love. It was my understanding of that scripture that helped me be abstinent for about five or six years after my divorce. It was that scripture that kept me single for almost fifteen years. After understanding that scripture, I just couldn't and still will not accept any type of treatment from a man. It is that scripture that causes me to say, "I like you and all, but you is not the one for me. Nope, you *is* not the one." I've been called stubborn and heartless, but that is far from the truth. I have found out what love is, and I am not going to settle for anything less than that. End of discussion. Let's understand this scripture together.

Though I speak with the tongues of men and angels, and have not charity, I am become as sounding brass, or a tinkling cymbal. And though I have the gift of prophecy, and understand all mysteries, and all knowledge; and though I have all faith, so that I could remove mountains, and have not charity, I am nothing. And though I bestow all my goods to feed the poor, and though I give my body to be burned, and have not charity, it profiteth me nothing. Charity suffereth long, and is kind; charity envieth not; charity vaunteth, not itself, is not puffed up. Doth not behave itself unseemly, seeketh not her own, is not easily provoked, thinketh no evil; Rejoiceth not in iniquity, but rejoiceth in the truth; Beareth all things, believeth all things, hopeth all things, endureth all things. Charity never faileth: but whether there be prophecies, they shall fail; whether there be tongues, they shall cease; whether there be knowledge, it shall vanish away. For we know in part, and we prophesy in part. But when that which is perfect is come, then that which is in part shall be done away. When I was a child, I spake as a child, I understood as a child, I thought as a child: but when I became a man, I put away childish things. For now, see through a glass, darkly; but then face to face: now I know in part; but then shall I know even as also I am known. And now abideth faith, hope, charity, these three; but the greatest of these is charity. (1 Corinthians 13)

Read this scripture over and over. Read every version you can find. Let God speak to your soul. Feel His love for you. Let Him explain how you should be treated. If you don't have love, what do you have? You can't give what you don't have. If you don't have love in your heart, you will not be able to give love to another. Love is long-suffering. Are you willing to put up with any and everything in a relationship? How long are you willing to stay? What will you not put up with? Love is kind. Do you always have something kind to say to your loved one? Do you tear them down with your words? Intentionally or unintentionally? Was it kind? Ask them if your words are always kind. Then ask yourself, are they lifting you up with their words? Do they show kindness toward you? Love is not jealous. You mean to tell me the sweet way he says, "Who is this dude?" doesn't mean he cares for you? No, it doesn't. Love is not jealous. It is as simple as that. Love is not puffed up. It is not arrogant. Seeketh not her own. It is not me, me, me. It is not "What you are doing for me?" It is not, "If you don't do this, then I am not going to love you anymore." It is not conditional. Where did you learn to love from? Does it line up with this scripture? Is the love you know now healthy? Can you compare it to this scripture? Is there a contrast to the love you know today? If you're married, compare the love between you and your spouse to this scripture. Get rid of everything that does not line up with this scripture. Can you look at yourself in the mirror and say you love yourself?

> Therefore there is now no condemnation [no guilty verdict, no punishment] for those who are in Christ Jesus [who believe in Him as personal Lord and Savior]. (Romans 8:1)

Why is it important for women to read a book like *Crowning Conversations?* Women need to not feel guilty about falling down and getting back up. Sometimes when you fall, the greatest comeback is getting back up. You will fall back into the old pattern if you don't address the issues. I heard Crystal say this in an interview and wanted to encourage you in it. When life knocks you down, don't feel ashamed or guilty. Yes, it is easier for me to say this on the other side of my getting up, but when you feel guilty or ashamed, it keeps you from getting the help you need. It keeps you mentally and emotionally drained. It keeps you from moving on and moving forward. Remember, you are not alone, and you are not the first and certainly won't be the last person who's been through what you've been through. Guilt is torment from the enemy, so let's get rid of guilt and shame. I heard in my spirit a long time ago "to get rid of a thing is to get to the root of a thing," so let's pull this thing up from the root so it can't hold you in bondage any longer.

- Admit out loud what mistake was made. Was the mistake truly your fault or the fault of someone else? It wasn't until about fifteen years after my divorce that I said what led up to my divorce—that I didn't know if I was blind to the fact that maybe I caused the straw to break the camel's back.
- Learn from your mistakes.

  I pray God your whole spirit and soul and body be preserved blameless unto the coming of our Lord Jesus Christ. (1 Thessalonians 5:23)

At church, we hear, "You are spirit, you possess a soul, and you live in a body." What is the connection of the mind, body, and spirit? To truly have/live the life God wants us to live, we cannot have one without the other two. It makes us who we are. As a spirit, we could not walk on the earth without our bodies. And without our minds, we could not function. Once the brain goes, our life is over.

The main concept behind the mind-body-spirit connection is that we are all more than just our thoughts. We are also our bodies, our emotions, and our spirituality ... all these things combine to give us identity, determine our health, and make us who we are. Mind-body-spirit means that our wellness comes not just from physical health, but from mental health and spiritual health as well. To be "healthy," we must pay attention to all three aspects of our nature. (Mind, Body, Spirit-E-Health Connection, March 24, 2020)

Let me give you some examples of mind-body-spirit connection:

The best feeling in the world for me is when I am in a worship service. I have been in a service where the presence of God was so strong that sometimes the Word could not be taught, because the Holy Ghost took over. We let go of insecurities and restraints and just praised and worshipped God. I let it all go during worship. This is the place where I can truly be transparent with God, telling Him my fears and concerns, letting Him know how much I love Him and appreciate who He is and what He does for me. This is another release for me, and my spirit is lifted and free from worry, condemnation, and negativity. I leave full of confidence, knowing God is my rock, my shield, my source, my protector, my way maker, my advocate. This list is endless. But this is where my spirit has connected with my mind and soul.

Another great feeling for me is right after I work out, especially one where I've lifted heavy weights. I feel like a beast. My confidence shoots through the roof. That is my mind connecting to the actions that took place in my body. This in turn makes my spirits high.

> For whoever finds me (Wisdom) finds life. And
> obtains favor and grace from the Lord. (Proverbs
> 8: 35 AMP)

Don't just haphazardly go through life. With all of your getting, get an understanding. Wisdom will save you from harm, keep you from making stupid mistakes, and save your life. Do all you can to gain wisdom.

This is one of the principles I live by. Don't be the person who has to hit the brick wall over and over again before you get a bump on your head. I am sure I learned this principle as a little girl, maybe five or six years old. I never liked being in trouble. I didn't like whippings. I wanted to stay as far away from them as possible. In fact, my siblings can attest when we were young and the question was asked, "Who did it?" I always had the answer. You see, when I was growing up, if someone didn't fess up, everyone would get a whipping, and I was not the one to catch another person's whipping. I also learned if I saw someone get in trouble for something, there was no way I would get in trouble for the same thing. Mistakes usually have a negative consequence, and if we learn from them, we tend not to repeat the mistake. This I have found over time is true wisdom.

Here are some tips:

- Read the Word daily. When I first began reading the Bible, I would read a chapter of Proverbs every day. Whatever date it was, that's the chapter I would read. I knew Proverbs was known as the Book of Wisdom, and I wanted to be full of wisdom.
- Pay attention to wisdom and instruction. Don't ignore it. Earlier, I said my daddy is wise. If I had listened to him when I was growing, it would have saved me a lot of heartache.

- Listen to wisdom daily. Today, there's no excuse for not obtaining wisdom. There's the Bible, Google, YouTube, and many social media platforms.
- Watch for wisdom daily. Learn from other people, not just their mistakes but their successes as well. You can learn a lot just by watching people.
- Wait for wisdom. Don't be quick to jump, especially in relationships. Take your time and wait for red flags to see if this is a good or bad one to get into.
- Seek God daily. Read the Word, listen to the Word, and meditate on the Word.

And the Lord said unto him, What is that in thine hand? (Exodus 4:2)

Be who God created you to be and do what God created you to do. Don't wait until everything is perfect to get started. Start now. Whatever God has been laying on your heart to do, just begin it. God called upon Moses to free His people from the Egyptians. God asked, "What is that in your hand?" God knew His power, but he was asking Moses, "What do you have I can use so my power can flow through you?" Moses had a rod. God used it to do many miracles, including parting the Red Sea. What miracles does God want to perform through you? Did you know Genesis 1:26 gave us authority, and God cannot do anything without us? He has to have a body to perform miracles through. Why not you? Yes you? You are what and who God needs. I didn't think so at first, but here I am writing to you to encourage you to use what you have in your hands, and God will create miracles. He will turn someone's life around because of you. He will empower someone because of you. He will heal someone because of you. But you have to be obedient and do what He tells you to do.

I used what I had in my hands. I didn't wait until I had my own studio. I didn't wait until I received that four-year degree. I didn't wait until I had fifty people to join my classes. I just began with what I had in my hands: my passion for dance and music and helping people reach their fitness goals. I still don't have my own studio, yet here I am, the coauthor of a best-selling book. You take the steps, do exactly what God lays on your heart to do, and God will open up the Red Sea for you. He will protect you from anything that will keep you from reaching your destiny and purpose. (Read Exodus 14.)

I encourage you to meditate on the following verses. They are all about God using what the people had in their hands and making a miracle. I was once told that when you pray, it is you speaking to God, but when you meditate, that is God speaking to you, showing you everything you can and will have if you just follow His lead. When you meditate on these scripture, write what you hear in your heart. God is speaking to you. Do what He tells you to do.

> When Jesus then lifted up his eyes, and saw a great company come unto him, he saith unto Philip, Whence shall we buy bread, that these may eat? And this he said to prove him: for he himself knew what he would do. Philip answered him, Two hundred pennyworth of bread is not sufficient for them, that every one of them may take a little. One of his disciples, Andrew, Simon Peter's brother, saith unto him, There is a lad here, which hath five barley loaves, and two small fishes: but what are they among so many? And Jesus said, Make the men sit down. Now there was much grass in the place. So the men sat down, in number about five thousand. And Jesus took the loaves; and when he had given thanks, he distributed to the disciples,

and the disciples to them that were set down; and likewise of the fishes as much as they would. When they were filled, he said unto his disciples, Gather up the fragments that remain, that nothing be lost. (John 6:5–12 KJV)

Now there cried a certain woman of the wives of the sons of the prophets unto Elisha, saying, Thy servant my husband is dead; and thou knowest that thy servant did fear the Lord: and the creditor is come to take unto him my two sons to be bondmen. And Elisha said unto her, What shall I do for thee? tell me, what hast thou in the house? And she said, Thine handmaid hath not any thing in the house, save a pot of oil. Then he said, Go, borrow thee vessels abroad of all thy neighbours, even empty vessels; borrow not a few. And when thou art come in, thou shalt shut the door upon thee and upon thy sons, and shalt pour out into all those vessels, and thou shalt set aside that which is full. So she went from him, and shut the door upon her and upon her sons, who brought the vessels to her; and she poured out. And it came to pass, when the vessels were full, that she said unto her son, Bring me yet a vessel. And he said unto her, There is not a vessel more. And the oil stayed. Then she came and told the man of God. And he said, Go, sell the oil, and pay thy debt, and live thou and thy children of the rest. 2 (Kings 4:1–7 KJV)

MEDITATION QUESTIONS:

1. What do you see? Write down everything you see.

2. What is the setting? What are the colors? Is it cold? Is it hot?

3. What is God's part?

4. What is your part?

5. What do you think God is saying to you from these scriptures? Read them several times and write everything you hear each time.

6. Is there anything about your character you need to change to match the character of the person(s) in the scripture? What can you cultivate? Sometimes we focus so much on the bad we forget about the good and sharpening that part of us so God can use it. For example, one of the coauthors of this book is a playwriter. She has other skills too, but she spends much of her time sharpening her playwriting skills. She goes to school, she attends other plays written by other people, she holds and attends workshops, and she holds table readings, all so she can sharpen her playwriting skills.

7. Is there anything you need to ask God to help you change or remove from your life? What about the little boy? Do you need to become more unselfish or giving like him?

I'm asking these questions to get you fully emerged in meditation. I want you to have good success according to Joshua 1:8.

THE DROP-OFF—THE PART OF THE JOURNEY WHERE PEOPLE GET OFF

But if ye forgive not men their trespasses, neither will your Father forgive your trespasses. (Matthew 6:15)

Forgiving and truly letting go is not for the other person; it is for you. This is one of those things that has to be pulled up by the root. Do whatever it takes to forgive. Unforgiveness will rot your soul. Let's walk through the process based on what God has to say about forgiveness.

- *Be kind, gentle, and forgiving.*
- *Forgive, and your Father in heaven will forgive you.* I don't know about you, but I have done some dirt intentionally and unintentionally, and I want to get it right with my Father in heaven. I want Him to forgive me, so I forgive others. It is not easy, but if God said it, then that's what we are going to do.
- *If we confess our sins, He will cleanse us of all unrighteousness.* I want to be clean and made whole. Remember the leprous man? Tear that thang from the root, Lord. Help me to become more holy like You. I want a pure and clean heart. I do not want guilt hanging over my head. When you don't confess your sins, the enemy tries to use it as a tactic to bring guilt and shame. Confess your sins to God, and when the time is right, ask God to help you confess your sins to others. Watch God move on your behalf, because He knows it is not easy to forgive.
- *Four hundred and ninety is the number of times we should forgive those who sin against us.* Are you really counting? If you are, then ask God to help you let it go. Are you keeping tabs to throw it in the other person's face? Let it go. I am not talking about if a person is physically, mentally, or emotionally abusing you. Get out of that relationship now. But I am talking about being petty. Be the bigger person and let it go.

- *Judge not, and you will not be judged.* Most of the time, I have found when people are judgmental, they are truly unhappy with themselves. They are the ones who find everything wrong with you to hide or cover up everything wrong with them.

- *Do good to those who hate you.* Kill them with kindness. This means no matter what they do, don't let them get you out of character. Keep being nice, show them favor, don't talk down to them, and be as positive as you can be. By doing this, the Bible says you heap burning coals on their heads. People don't know how to respond to this type of treatment, and it usually makes them either treat you the same way they are treating you, or it makes them stop and walk away. I've seen it happen too many times in my life. People think I am weak because I am kind. Oh, baby, don't mistake my kindness for weakness, because in reality, a beast lives inside of me, and you don't want her to come out.

- *Love covers all offenses.* Love will have you overlook others' faults. Don't argue or discuss private things in public. Find a way to calmly talk out differences of opinion. Write letters. Send emails. Whatever you do, don't air your dirty laundry.

- *Repent.* To repent means to express sincere regret or remorse about one's wrongdoing. It is to see the error of one's ways. It is also followed by a change of actions. When a person truly repents, he/she will change the actions that caused the hurt or offense.

DESTINATION: THE FINISH LINE

Let us not grow weary or become discouraged in doing good, for at the proper time we will reap, if we do not give in. (Galatians 6:9 AMP)

Whatever you do, finish strong. It is important to finish what you start and finish strong. When I began working out, my body would give up quickly, and I would complete only half of the workout. I began to tell myself before a workout, "No matter what we are doing, I'm going to complete at least two rounds of each block." And I would press through until the end. Sometimes the coach would begin another block and I would have a few more reps to go. I would finish the round I was in and then begin the next one. It was important to me to finish and finish strong. You can relate this to any task you begin, but I am going to relate it to working out for illustration purposes. What gets you through a workout? If you're having a hard time, here are some tips to help you make it through:

- *Remain focused.* Remind yourself why you are doing this and what you need to do to do it well. Is the reason you're working out health related? Is it for you to reduce stress? If you remember your why during your workout, you are guaranteed to finish strong.
- *Prepare yourself mentally.* Tell your mind what it wants to hear, and your body will follow. Recite the affirmations from the previous pages. Tell yourself you can do this. Listen to the words of music playing and make positive statements to repeat to yourself. Do this until the workout is complete.
- *Set the scene.* Visualize the challenges you'll face and picture how you will respond to them. Mental imagery and meditation are powerful. The bible says in Genesis 11 nothing can be restrained from them which they imagined to do. As I stated earlier, see imagine) yourself as finishing strong. Determine what finishing strong means to you. Maybe it's just to run a mile. Maybe it's to complete two rounds. Whatever it is, decide beforehand and get it done. When I first began running on the treadmill, I did not like

to run. I had to keep reminding myself this is the part of the workout that makes the heart and lungs stronger. Also pretend you're somewhere else while you're working out. If you are running on a treadmill, picture yourself running on a beach or running from a dog—whatever works for you to make it through the workout.

- *Keep track of how you're doing.* Track your progression. For example, when I began on the treadmill, I couldn't run two minutes without stopping. Then I noticed I was running three minutes, then five, then eight, and so on, nonstop. There are many fitness tracking devices available today to assist you in your journey.

- *Don't think about what you're going through.* Think about the goal, the end results, the fact you're actually moving forward. This will free your mind of unnecessary clutter while working out.

- *Break it up.* For me to do a high number of reps, I have to do them in sets. For example, if the rep count is twenty, I may do two sets of ten or four sets of five, depending on the exercise and weight.

- *Tune in.* Tune in to the mind-muscle connection. Take note of your breathing and what your muscles are actually doing. This can also help push you through a workout. Focusing on your body can take stress off the workout. Take note of your form, especially when you begin to fatigue. We can lose form when we are tired.

- *Tune out.* Focusing on anything but the workout can help you push through. Work through a problem or recall a happy memory. Counting your steps while you walk or run can also help.

- *Self-talk.* David encouraged himself. It is OK to be your own cheerleader.

- *Know better is yet to come.* Know what's on the other side of the race/workout. Every rep counts. You are going to get better, stronger, healthier, and more fit.
- *Smile.* When you smile, you feel more positive and less psychological pain. The more you smile, the more the crowd will smile back. It infuses positive energy.
- *Stop.* If you're injured, stop. If you need water, stop. If you're in pain, stop. Tune into your body over everything else.

And let the maiden which pleaseth the king be queen instead of Vashti. (Esther 2:4)

Let me sum up the story of Queen Esther in one sentence. The king called for her to come; she did not come, so she lost her crown. Point. Blank. Period. Don't lose your crown by not showing up. When you consistently make an effort to show up and do what is required of you, you will go up. For instance, let's take reading the Bible. If you consistently show up and meet God in your Bible-reading time and apply what you are reading to your life, then you will go up. Scriptures say your mind will be renewed and your life will be transformed. Myles Munroe, a famous teacher of the Gospel, once said that once you learn new information, your life is changed forever. If you are showing up and reading and applying what you have learned to your life, you too will go up. On the other hand, if you disregard showing up because maybe you're too tired or you just don't feel like it, you in essence skip out on your go up.

"It is written" (Luke 4:4).

I was once told, "If you can read, you can do anything." I encourage you to become an avid reader. The words "it is written" are listed ninety-five times in the King James Version of the Bible. Jesus Himself said many times, "It is written." In order for Him to know what is written, He had to read what was written. Jesus was an avid reader. Find topics you like and read. If you find it hard to sit down and read, listen to audiobooks. I listen to audiobooks while going to and from work. I also listen to them while cleaning. I listen to them while I soak in the tub after a hard workout. A well-known rapper, Nipsey Hussle, would listen to them while he slept. When I was a young girl, I loved it so much I preferred reading over going outside to play. I don't know why or when I let that habit go, but I am picking it back up and reading as much as possible.

Reading …

- increases your vocabulary
- helps you become more knowledgeable
- helps you become a better communicator
- will inspire you to become a better you

> Now that I am old and my hair is gray, don't leave me, God. I must tell the next generation about your power and greatness. (Psalm 71:18–19)

Colonel Sanders, born Harland David Sanders, was born September 9, 1890. He began cooking at age five or six after his father died and his mother had to work to make money for the family. He was the oldest of three children and had to take care of himself and siblings while his mom worked. But it wasn't until he was sixty-two years old in 1952 that he opened his first Kentucky Fried Chicken. And look at where Kentucky Fried Chicken is today. In the Bible, Sarah was ninety-nine when she became pregnant with Isaac. But age is just a number when it comes to the purpose God has for you. So don't think you're too old to live out your dreams, God's plans for your life. Get it started. Ask God for wisdom and believe He will give you the resources needed to get the job done. Also let me encourage you in this. If you know starting a business is not for you, maybe your purpose is to spread the Gospel. Social media is a great place for spreading the Word. Maybe your purpose is to write blogs on God's power and greatness. God created you for a purpose. The aforementioned scripture may be for you.

> Thou wilt keep him in perfect peace, whose mind is stayed on thee: because he trusteth in thee. (Isaiah 26:3)

What does the Bible say about peace? In lieu of today's pandemic, is it even possible to have and keep a peace of mind? More than nine million people tested positive for COVID, and 229,000 people died of the disease in the USA alone. (Worldwide: 44.9 million cases and 1.18 million deaths.) Older adults and people who have severe underlying medical conditions like heart or lung disease or diabetes seem to be at higher risk for developing more serious complications from COVID-19. Children are being homeschooled, and unemployment is over 10 percent. It would behoove me to talk about how to have peace of mind. Here are a few scriptures, and below them is exactly what to do or not to do when it comes to having peace of mind. According to the Word of God, you should …

- *Pray about everything.* This means each item, each thing, every single thing, the whole lot, leaving out nothing.
- *Know that God gives us peace.* The Bible says He's the Prince of Peace; of course we can have what he has.
- *Cast your burdens on the Lord.* To cast means to throw, toss, pitch, hurl.
- *Get a good word in your heart.* What does the Word of God say about the situation that tries to stress you out? Pray the scripture and make affirmations. Get the Word of God

settled on that thing in your heart so the enemy cannot bring dark thoughts into your mind about it.

- *Don't fear.* "Fear not" is listed in the King James Version of the Bible 170 times. Now imagine God speaking directly to you and saying over and over again, "Fear not," 170 times. Talk about a shift in emotions and mindset. If you're old enough, you'll remember when we had to write on the chalkboard or on a piece of paper one hundred times "I will not talk in class" or whatever you were in trouble for. Try writing "I will not fear" one hundred times on a sheet of paper or in your journal, since I know you'll start one soon after completing this book.

- *Go to God.* Most of us go to our friends when we need to talk, but have you tried to go to God before you talk to your friends?

- *Know that God is for you.*

- *Remain steadfast to the things of God.*

- *Don't fuss too much and get yourself worked up over nothing.* I am not making light of COVID or the pandemic, but in this instance, don't get worked up over simple things. In other words, don't make mountains out of anthills.

- *Don't forget God's benefits.* The Bible says He daily loads us with benefits. Just what are those benefits? Research it. Read the Bible to find out His benefits and remind yourself daily of them.

- *Let not your hearts be troubled.*

- *Have a strong foundation.* Know the Word and promises of God.

- *Believe in God.*

I didn't realize it until now, but God was keeping me in perfect peace by helping me to stay focused on Him. Every crowning conversation I had led me back to God and His Word. My life, my journey, was to bring me to a point of not just any kind of peace but perfect peace. And that is just like God to do exceeding, abundantly above all I can ask, think, imagine, guess, request, or conjure up in wildest dreams. He didn't push me into it; He helped me through the journey—purging me, cleansing me, delivering me, protecting me, and keeping me. Glory to God. He is able.

MEET THE AUTHORS

Deidra is a native Houstonian, God-fearing wife, mother of two (2), leader in Criminal Justice, Realtor (TeamLead), Amazon Best-Selling Author, and Podcaster. She is the queen of discipline and execution.

www.ewingliving.com

IG: Deidra_Ewing

Yvette Cornish, MA, LPC, a self-proclaimed raptivist, is a licensed psychotherapist, motivational speaker, entrepreneur, and community activist. Visit her online at www.genesisblu.com.

Patrina Randolph, CLC, BFA, is a writer, producer, director, and entrepreneur. Visit her online at www.thefierceartsgroup.com.

Felishia Brown, CLC, BA, an NASM certified personal trainer, is CEO of Maximized Motions, Beastra, and Beastra Athletic Wear and currently coaches at Orange Theory Fitness. Visit her online at www.maximizedmotions.com.

CPSIA information can be obtained
at www.ICGtesting.com
Printed in the USA
BVHW071250291221
625052BV00016B/557